JOHN STUART
EARL OF BUTE

John Stuart, Earl of Bute

JOHN STUART
EARL OF BUTE

BY

J. A. LOVAT-FRASER, M.A.

OF TRINITY COLLEGE, CAMBRIDGE, AND THE INNER TEMPLE,
BARRISTER-AT-LAW

CAMBRIDGE:
AT THE UNIVERSITY PRESS
1912

CAMBRIDGE
UNIVERSITY PRESS

University Printing House, Cambridge CB2 8BS, United Kingdom

Cambridge University Press is part of the University of Cambridge.

It furthers the University's mission by disseminating knowledge in the pursuit of
education, learning and research at the highest international levels of excellence.

www.cambridge.org
Information on this title: www.cambridge.org/9781316613078

First published 1912
First paperback edition 2016

A catalogue record for this publication is available from the British Library

ISBN 978-1-316-61307-8 Paperback

TO

MY CHIEF,

SIMON JOSEPH FRASER,

FOURTEENTH

LORD LOVAT

CONTENTS

CHAPTER I

OVER a hundred and thirty years ago a party of diners sat round a table in a brilliantly lighted apartment in London. The tall candles burnt in their sconces, illuminating the glittering crystal and abundant decanters of the eighteenth century. At the head of the table sat the host, the leonine Lord Thurlow, with his growling voice and his bushy black eyebrows. The conversation fell upon Lord Bute, who some time before had retired from public office. One of the guests remarked that a Life of Lord Bute was going to be written. The surly host dismissed the information with the ill-natured comment, "the life of a fly would be as interesting."

In spite of Lord Thurlow's dictum, the career of John Stuart, Earl of Bute, is one of great interest, and full of instruction. He was the first Scotsman who attained the position of Prime Minister of the United Kingdom of Great Britain. He was the chief adviser of George the Third from his accession till April, 1763. During that time he brought upon himself an amount of hatred and detestation rarely equalled in English history. While in office he was probably the most unpopular minister that ever served an English monarch. He was *le parvenu montagnard*, the upstart Highlander, as a contemporary pamphlet called him, who was regarded as bringing from Scotland all the evil traditions

of the Stuart race. When he retired, he was still the
object of unscrupulous abuse and unfounded slander.
For long years after his fall, he was pictured as the evil
genius of the sovereign, ever whispering traitorous
counsels in his ear, and prompting him to every kind of
unconstitutional proceeding. He was made the scapegoat
for the blunders of ministers who were in reality his
bitterest opponents. It was his fate to

> " Live to be the show and gaze o' the time,
> Painted upon a pole ; and underwrit,
> ' Here you may see the tyrant.' "

Bute was the representative of one of the noble
Scottish families who trace their descent to the royal
house of Scotland. He was descended from Sir John
Stewart, who was the natural son of King Robert the
Second, and who was appointed Sheriff of Bute in 1385
by his father. The chief seat of the family was the little
Island of Bute in the Firth of Clyde. Here, under the
heather-clad mountains of Argyllshire, the ancestors of
the future Prime Minister had dwelt for generations.
Rothesay, the little burgh town on the north side of the
island, was an old home of the royal house. King
Robert the Third had died in the castle, which still
stands in ruins in the centre of the town, and the
eldest son of each Scottish monarch bore the title of
Duke of Rothesay. In modern days Rothesay is a
cluster of common-place streets and villas, the dumping
ground on to which grimy Glasgow and the industrial
centres of the West of Scotland pour their crowds of
excursionists during the summer holidays. In Bute's
time the island was still a secluded spot outside the
sphere of Lowland influence. It was frequented by few
travellers, and inhabited by a scanty population, who

spoke Gaelic. Bute himself was regarded as a High-lander, and, as already mentioned, a contemporary satirical history described him as " Le Montagnard Parvenu, or the New Highland Adventurer in England."

The subject of this book was born on 25th May 1713, and was the son of James, second Earl of Bute, by Anne Campbell, the daughter of Archibald, first Duke of Argyll. He was born, not in Bute, but in the Parliament Square of Edinburgh, a spot saturated with the most inspiring traditions of Scottish history, and consecrated to national feeling by a statue of King Charles the Second. Within a stone's throw of his birthplace stood the halls where the Parliament of Scotland had met before the Union, and where the burning eloquence of Fletcher and Belhaven had been echoed by enthusiastic applause. The custom of sending boys of the Scottish aristocracy to English schools had already commenced, and Bute went to Eton for his education. In 1736, when twenty-three years of age, he married Mary, the daughter of the famous and eccentric Lady Mary Wortley Montagu, by Edward Wortley Montagu of Wortley in Yorkshire. Lady Mary was strongly opposed to the union, but the bride went her own way, and wedded the man she loved.

The marriage proved a happy one. Lord Chesterfield says, in his *Character* of Bute, that he made a run-away love-match, but notwithstanding lived very happily with his wife. Twelve years afterwards Lady Mary, the mother of Lady Bute, wrote to her husband : " What I think extraordinary is my daughter's continuing so many years agreeable to Lord Bute ; Mr Mackenzie telling me, the last time I saw him, that his brother frequently said among his companions, that he was as

much in love with his wife as before he married her."
Lady Mary quite forgot in later years, as other mothers
have done in similar circumstances, that she had violently
opposed her daughter's marriage.   "You give Lord
Bute," she wrote, in 1742, to her husband, "the character
I always believed belonged to him from the first of our
acquaintance, and the opinion I had of his honesty
(which is the most essential quality) made me so easily
consent to the match."   Lady Bute seems to have been
a woman of great prudence and tact, and, even when her
husband's fortunes were at the highest, was always wise
and discreet.   It is a high tribute to her that she was
a favourite of the notorious and then aged Sarah Jen-
nings, Duchess of Marlborough, and was one of the few
persons with whom the Duchess never quarrelled.

Bute, like Cromwell, did not become famous till
middle age, and it is unnecessary to linger over his early
life.   He was elected a Scottish representative peer in
1737, but was not re-elected to the Parliament of 1741,
and twenty years passed before he again appeared in
the House of Lords.   Although he ultimately acquired
a large fortune by his wife, his early married life was
hampered by poverty.   Poverty dogged the footsteps of
most of the Scots nobility, and Bute but shared the
common lot of his class.   He was compelled to spend
the first nine years after his marriage in an economical
retirement in the Island of Bute.   In the early part of
1746 he appears to have been in some financial em-
barrassment owing to the falling of stocks, the general
scarcity consequent on the war, and a terrible murrain
that had then made havoc among the cattle.   About
this time he left Scotland, and came to Twickenham, on
the banks of the Thames.   In March, 1746, Edward

Wortley Montagu wrote to his wife, Lady Mary, that Bute had "for the next year taken the house which was Mr Stone's for £45 a year, which you will think extremely cheap. She (Lady Bute) tells me they design to lay down their coach, and that Scotch estates bring little to London." Bute was a man of culture, and a student, and in the seclusion of his Scottish home had found congenial occupation in the study of mathematics, mechanics and botany. He continued his eccentric pursuits in his new domicile, and the future Prime Minister might have been seen looking for specimens among the fields and hedges on the banks of the Thames.

About 1747 the quiet life of Bute was broken by an important event. He made the acquaintance of Frederick, Prince of Wales, an occurrence which laid the foundation of his fortunes. Mrs Boscawen, widow of the celebrated Admiral Boscawen, told Sir Nathaniel Wraxall that the introduction was quite accidental. Bute visited the Egham races, and, not having a carriage of his own, drove to the course in the chariot of the apothecary who attended his family. Prince Frederick, who then resided at Cliefden, happened to be present at the races, and, the weather proving rainy, it was proposed to have a game of cards in a tent that had been erected for his accommodation. A difficulty occurred about finding persons of sufficient rank to play with the Prince, until somebody suggested that Lord Bute, whose rank as an Earl entitled him to form one of the party, had been seen on the course. Bute was introduced to the Prince, and joined in the game. After it was over, it was discovered that the apothecary had gone, and in the difficulty, the Prince insisted that Bute should accompany him to Cliefden, and pass the night there. Bute complied, and thereby laid the foundation of his friendship with the Prince, and of his future eminence.

Bute soon became a constant *habitué* of the Royal circle at Cliefden and Worcester House. Frederick, who was affable and good-tempered, but weak and frivolous, was fond of private theatricals. Bute had acted in Young's *Revenge* at Queensberry House, where the Duchess of Queensberry had organised amateur performances. He had also filled the part of "Castalio" in Otway's *Orphan* so well that Frederick had asked that it might be performed before him. Bute was invited to join in the amateur performances at the Royal entertainments and, it is said, frequently played the part of "Lothario." He was a handsome man, and his enemies said that, like Sim Tappertit in *Barnaby Rudge*, he particularly admired the symmetry of his own legs, and liked to display them on the amateur stage. His intimacy with the Prince brought him and his wife out of the retirement in which they had hitherto lived, and ambitions, hitherto dormant, made themselves felt. They began to play a more prominent part in the great world. "Lord Bute and my daughter's conduct," wrote Lady Mary Wortley Montagu, "may be owing to the advice of the Duke of Argyll. It was a maxim of Sir R. Walpole's that whoever expected advancement should appear much in public. He used to say, whoever neglected the world, would be neglected by it, though I believe more families have been ruined than raised by that method." In September, 1750, Bute received official standing by being appointed Lord of the Bedchamber to Prince Frederick.

In 1751 Prince Frederick died. Lady Mary Wortley Montagu anticipated that this event would have a bad

effect on the fortunes of her son-in-law, and gave vent
to fears, which were not, however, justified. " I suppose,"
she wrote, " Prince George will have a household fixed,
and methinks his father's servants should have preference.
However that is, the disappointment must still be very
great to Lord Bute. I do not doubt his hopes were very
high. *Nescia mens hominum fati sortisque futurae.* As
I have a good opinion of his honesty, I think it is a
national misfortune that he has lost the prospect of
having a share in the confidence of a king." Bute,
however, continued his friendship with the Princess.
He was constantly at her house, and was consulted by
her in all her concerns. The world, always ready to be
uncharitable, asserted that an immoral connexion united
the two; an allegation which in later days became an
article of faith with Bute's enemies. Shelburne hints
that Bute first formed an illicit connexion with Lady
Howe, who was Lady of the Bedchamber, and afterwards
threw her over for the Princess. " I believe it's certain,"
says Shelburne, " that Lady Howe at last forgave him.
Though old and ugly, she conceived she had a right to
his constancy, and was not disposed to yield it very
willingly to her mistress."

The friendship between Bute and the Princess had
one not unnatural result. George, the eldest son of the
Princess and heir to the throne, was growing up, and
Bute acquired a powerful influence over the young man.
George was kept in seclusion, in order to preserve him,
so his mother said, from the evil influences that surrounded him. It was asserted in after years, however,
that the Princess and Bute, adopting the treatment
accorded to the youthful Louis the Fourteenth by Anne
of Austria and Cardinal Mazarin, deliberately kept him

in a state of tutelage, that they might secure the power, when he should come to the throne. In 1756, when the Prince was eighteen years of age, the King decided to give him an establishment of his own. Bute was appointed Groom of the Stole and head of the Prince's household, but not without much wire-pulling and considerable difficulty. A full account of the negotiations which preceded the appointment are given in Von Ruville's splendid work on Chatham, and it is unnecessary to detail them here. George the Second was most unwilling to place Bute at the head of the Prince's establishment. He resented the influence which the Princess Dowager and Bute enjoyed with Prince George, and the Prince had himself to urge the appointment on the King. "Nothing," he wrote, "could make me happier or fill my mind with warmer gratitude than your Majesty's gracious consent in favour of a character, an early and long acquaintance with whom has naturally won my high esteem, and of whose devotion and zeal for your Majesty I am most firmly convinced."

When the King at length consented to the appointment of Bute, he did it grudgingly, and refused to admit him into the closet to receive the badge of his office. He gave it to the Duke of Grafton, who slipped the gold key into the Scottish nobleman's pocket, whispering to him not to resent the affront—a piece of advice which Bute prudently accepted. When Bute appeared to kiss hands, the King declined to vouchsafe him a single word, and he subsequently reproached Henry Fox for forcing on him the appointment of that " puppy " Bute as Groom of the Stole. The other appointments to the Prince's household were left to the Prime Minister, Newcastle, and it affords an interesting light on the prevailing methods of government that no less than ten individuals received office, who were members of one or other House of Parliament, in order that their votes might be secured for the administration. Lady Mary was naturally gratified at the elevation of her son-in-law, and wrote to her daughter, wishing her joy of her new situation. " Lord Bute," she wrote, "has attained it by a very uncommon road; I mean an acknowledged honour and probity. I have but one short instruction (pardon the word) to give on his account; that he will never forget the real interest of Prince and people cannot be divided, and are almost as closely united as that of soul and body." It was now fully recognised that Bute was a coming man, and the comparative merits of Newcastle, the actual Prime Minister, and Bute, who might possibly be Prime Minister in the future, were widely discussed. The witty Charles Townshend, who was related to both, flippantly dismissed the subject, " silly fellow for silly fellow, I think it is as well to be governed by my uncle, with a blue riband, as by my cousin, with a green one."

As a result of Bute's influence with the Princess Dowager, the education of Prince George was left in his hands. Bute was a Tory, and the Prince's education was conducted on Tory lines. The prevailing form of government at that time was oligarchical Whiggery. Since the accession of George the First in 1714 a few Whig families, by dint of corruption and borough influence, had secured all the power. The majority of the House of Commons were returned by the Whig nobles. The long exclusion of the Tories from office had tended to lessen the influence of the Crown. England, to use Disraeli's historic comparison, was governed on Venetian principles. The Whig magnificoes, who corresponded to the Venetian aristocrats, had reduced the King to the level of a Doge. The throne was "a mere pageant," to use Lord Shelburne's words. The King was allowed to do as he pleased within the limits of his Court, but he was never suffered to take part in the actual conduct of affairs. Public corruption was the chief instrument of government, and, as might have been expected, inefficiency and incompetence were the order of the day. Any fool may rule under a system of corruption. "A chambermaid," said Bolingbroke, "may slip a banknote into a griping paw as well as the most subtle demon of hell." No great ability was required for the post of Prime Minister when his chief duty was to supervise a system of bribery, and the Whigs were able to make their nominee, the Duke of Newcastle, virtually sovereign of England, although he was, as Disraeli justly described him, "the most incompetent of men."

George was educated to regard the existing Whig *régime* with strong hostility. It was said that George Scott, the Prince's sub-preceptor, was recommended by Bolingbroke. Andrew Stone, the sub-governor, who was a brother of Archbishop Stone, the Primate of Ireland, and a distinguished Oxford scholar, was accused of Jacobitism, and of drinking the health of "The King over the water." He was charged with having given the Prince Archdeacon Echard's translation of the *Revolutions d'Angleterre* by Père d'Orleans, a book written in defence of James the Second and his unconstitutional measures. Cresset, the Princess's secretary and favourite, who was related to Eleanor d'Emiers or d'Olbreuse, the wife of George William, Duke of Zell, and grandmother of George the Second, was also accused of influencing the mind of the Prince in an unconstitutional direction. It was said that the heir apparent had read several works which were anathematised by the Whigs and, amongst them, Ramsay's *Travels of Cyrus*, Sir Robert Filmer's *Patriarch*, and Père Perefixe's *History of Henry the Fourth*. The charges against Scott, Stone, and Cresset, were investigated, and declared to be without foundation, but there is little doubt that the Princess Dowager surrounded her son with an atmosphere of Toryism. The Princess, who had been reared in a despotic German Court, was all for prerogative, and influenced Prince George in the same direction. The Prince studied Bolingbroke's *Patriot King*, with its high views of regal power, and Bute procured a considerable portion of the manuscript of Blackstone's *Commentaries*, not then published, for the Prince's instruction. Blackstone's work was not less acceptable to Bute, because the definition of the king's authority, as set forth in the *Commentaries*, savoured of an earlier age, and was not one that the Whigs could endorse. The Prince was taught that the ideals at which he ought to aim were those set forth by Bolingbroke. He was to govern the people by his own will, but for their good. He was to be the pivot, round which the business of the nation was to move. He was to trample bribery and corruption under foot. He was to take the initiative in government and was to select his ministers from all parties. He was to be above parties and factions, and was to prevent the administration of the country from being monopolised by any one of them.

CHAPTER II

IN 1760 George obtained the opportunity of putting into practice the political principles in which he had been instructed. George the Second died, and Bute's pupil succeeded to the Crown. The Prince was riding from Kew to London on 25th October 1760, when a man on horseback accosted him and told him that the King had been suddenly seized by an attack of illness, which threatened to be fatal. The rider produced as his credentials "a piece of very coarse white-brown paper" containing merely the name of "Schrieder," a German valet of the late King. George was, according to Wraxall, accompanied by Bute at the time, and on the receipt of the news he at once returned to Kew. Later in the day a message came from the Princess Amelia announcing that the King was dead. George at once proceeded to London, and, on the way, met Pitt, who formally announced to him his accession to the throne.

Evidence of the influence of Bute was immediately given. Within a few hours of the death of George the Second a message was sent to the Duke of Newcastle commanding his presence at Carlton House. The Duke was received by Bute, and, when he entered the Royal closet, the King told him, "My Lord Bute is your good friend; he will tell you my thoughts." The declaration which the King proposed to make to the Privy Council was read to Newcastle, Pitt, and Holderness. It is said to have been written by the King himself with the help of Bute, and, after describing the war with France, which was then raging, as "bloody and expensive," expressed a desire for "an honourable and lasting peace." Pitt considered that those words were aimed at his military policy, and was furious. He at once went to Bute and, after a long altercation, obtained a change in the sentence. The declaration was read by the King to the Privy Council at Carlton House next day. The words actually used at the Council were : " As I mount the throne in the midst of an expensive, but just and necessary war, I shall endeavour to prosecute it in a manner most likely to bring about an honourable and lasting peace in concert with my allies."

The Whigs were quickly forced to recognise that a new order of things was at hand. Bute was made a Privy Councillor, and received the post of Ranger of Richmond Park in succession to the Princess Amelia. The name of the Duke of Cumberland, " The Butcher " of Highland tradition, so odious to all Scottish Tories, was struck out of the liturgy. Evidence of the power behind the throne was soon forthcoming. On the nineteenth of November the King delivered his first speech to Parliament. The speech was the composition of the Earl of Hardwicke, but the King had added certain memorable words of his own. " Born and educated in this country," said George, " I glory in the name of *Briton*, and the particular happiness of my life will ever consist in promoting the welfare of a people, whose loyalty and warm affection to me I consider the greatest and most permanent security of my throne." It is said that the King had originally written " Englishman," but Bute who, of course, was not an Englishman, had induced

him to alter it to "Briton[1]." The significance of the word
was not lost on the political world. The Duke of
Newcastle wrote to Lord Hardwicke, "I suppose you
will think 'Briton' remarkable. It denotes the author
to all the world." In using the word "Briton" as
distinguished from Englishman, most reasonable men
will admit that the King was only doing justice to his
Scottish and Irish subjects. Yet it was long before the
English forgave their sovereign for his use of the more
comprehensive term.

The King, having attained the throne, endeavoured
to put into practice the ideals which he had formed.
He proposed to act the part of the Patriot King. He
desired to substitute a real royalty for the chief magis-
tracy, to which the Whigs had reduced the kingly office.
He set before himself, as his chief aims, the emancipation
of the sovereign from ministerial tyranny, the abolition
of corruption at elections, and the abolition of government by party or connexion. He was determined to be
monarch in fact as well as in name. Kit Marlowe asks
in *Edward the Second*—

> "But what are kings, when regiment is gone,
> But perfect shadows in a sunshine day?"

George was resolved to be no shadow. His first proceeding was to remodel the cabinet. On 22nd March
1761, Henry Legge, the Chancellor of the Exchequer,
was dismissed, and William, Viscount Barrington took
his place. It was said that Legge was dismissed because
he refused a year and a half before to give place to
Sir Simeon Stuart, a Scotchman and a Jacobite, whom
Bute wished to bring in for Hampshire. Whether or

[1] The word actually used was "Britain." Many jokes were made
about the spelling of it.

not this is true, the King certainly regarded the fallen minister with little favour. When he handed his resignation to the King, he assured him that his future life should testify to his zeal for his Majesty's service. " I am glad of it," replied the King, " for nothing but your future life can eradicate the ill impression which I have received of you." On 25th March, Lord Holderness, Secretary of State for the Northern Department, was dismissed, and his post was given to Bute, who appointed as his under-secretary Charles Jenkinson, who himself afterwards became Prime Minister and Earl of Liverpool. The King told Rose in 1804 that he had been induced to appoint Bute on the recommendation of the Dukes of Newcastle and Devonshire, two of the Whig magnificoes. The Whig dukes may have said something to the King about appointing Bute, but there is little doubt that he would have received office, whether he had been recommended or not. He himself, however, was not anxious for ministerial position, and Chatham had consistently opposed his appointment to office, believing amongst other reasons that his nationality would make him unpopular. Bute's accession to the ministry was accompanied by two events, which considerably strengthened his position. One was the death of his uncle, the Duke of Argyll, whose power and influence in Scotland descended to himself. The other was the death of his father-in-law, Wortley Montagu, who left to Lady Bute an enormous fortune, which was estimated at £1,340,000.

The Tories heartily supported the King in his efforts to break up the Whig phalanx, which had so long controlled the crown. In the reaction against Whiggism foolish things were said and done. The divine right of Kings was again preached from the pulpit. The *North*

Briton held up to ridicule a divine named Trusler, who publicly maintained from the pulpit, that to resist the minister was to resist the King; to resist the King was to resist God, and that the consequence of such resistance must be damnation. Prerogative, as Horace Walpole relates, once more became a fashionable word. The great Jacobite families, who had long been absent from court, now crowded to the Palace. Lady Susan Stuart, daughter of the Earl of Galloway, who was, according to Walpole, "a notorious and intemperate Jacobite," was appointed Lady of the Bedchamber to the Princess Augusta, the King's eldest sister. "Lord Litchfield and several other Jacobites have kissed hands," wrote Horace Walpole on 13th November 1760. "George Selwyn says, 'they go to St James's, because now there are so many Stuarts there.'" Miss Katherine Dashwood, an intimate friend of Bute, reappeared at Court after an absence of a quarter of a century. "It is comical," writes Walpole, "to see Kitty Dashwood, the famous old beauty of the Oxfordshire Jacobites, living in the palace as duenna to the Queen."

The objects of the King had much to recommend them. It was felt that the chances of the Stuart dynasty were hopeless, and that the old divisions of Whig and Jacobite had ceased to have any meaning. It was considered highly detrimental to the public service that able and loyal politicians should be excluded from a share in the government, because they belonged, very often on hereditary grounds only, to a party opposed to the Whig connexion. Douglas, afterwards Bishop of Salisbury, probably inspired by Pulteney, Earl of Bath, who was his patron, issued a pamphlet in which the views of the Tories were shadowed forth.

The pamphlet was published in March 1761 and was entitled *Seasonable Hints from an Honest Man of the Present Important Crisis of a New Reign and a New Parliament.* Burke afterwards ridiculed the *Seasonable Hints* in his *Thoughts on the Causes of the Present Discontents*, and gave a sarcastic description of the policy of the Tories. Burke's description, satirical though it is, is a not inapt account of the objects of Bute and his friends. "Party," wrote Burke, "was to be totally done away with, with all its evil works. Corruption was to be cast down from Court, as Atè was from heaven. Power was thenceforward to be the chosen residence of public spirit; and no one was to be supposed under any sinister influence, except those who had the misfortune to be in disgrace at court, which was to stand in lieu of all vices and all corruptions. A scheme of perfection to be realised in a monarchy, far beyond the visionary Republic of Plato....Now was the time to unlock the sealed fountain of Royal bounty, which had been infamously monopolised and huckstered, and to let it flow at large upon the whole people. The time was come to restore Royalty to its original splendour. *Mettre le Roy hors de page*[1] became a sort of watchword."

When Bute entered the Cabinet the Prime Minister was Thomas Pelham, Duke of Newcastle, but its most dominant personality was William Pitt. To describe the character of one so well known as this great statesman is unnecessary. Pitt was emphatically "a man, un homme," as Frederick the Great called him. Amidst the politicians of his time he was, as Disraeli once said, "a forest oak in a suburban garden." Of undaunted

[1] "To bring the king out of guardianship."

courage, fertile in resources, his one aim was the glory
of his country. To him may be applied the words
which Lord Salisbury used of Disraeli, " Zeal for the
greatness of England was the passion of his mind."
Nothing affords a better insight into his nature than the
fact that he was willing to pardon a fault that was the
result of excessive daring, but never one that was the
result of undue caution. Finding himself amidst a crowd
of mediocrities, he was overbearing and imperious. The
Cabinet existed merely to register his decrees, and
Newcastle freely admitted that the whole Council
dreaded his frown. As long as Pitt was in the Cabinet,
Bute was necessarily a secondary figure. The course of
events, however, soon led to Pitt's retirement.

When George the Third mounted the throne in 1760,
the Seven Years' War was running its course. France
had been reduced to a state of abject distress. Her
financial condition was desperate. Her navy was
ruined. The peasantry were pressed into the service
on the sea to such an extent that women might be
seen in the fields of France handling the plough. The
success of the British arms had been largely due to
Pitt, who had conducted the war with the greatest ability,
and had acquired great glory by his management of it.
Negotiations had taken place in 1761 between Pitt and
the French Minister, Choiseul, with a view to peace on
the basis of *uti possidetis*, each country to keep what it
had taken. But Pitt had declared that Great Britain
would not desert her ally, the King of Prussia, and
the negotiations came to nothing. Pitt was resolved
to continue the contest till he obtained terms which
he considered satisfactory. A new development in
the situation, however, altered his plans. The King of

France, crushed and humiliated, made a secret treaty with Charles the Third, King of Spain, by which the two Bourbon monarchs engaged to unite against England. Pitt, hearing of the treaty, called in an imperious manner for immediate and vigorous measures against Spain as well as France. Bute opposed the declaration of war against Spain, and carried his colleagues with him. Pitt, finding that his views were not accepted by the Cabinet, resigned on 5th October 1761. He refused, he said, to remain in a situation which made him responsible for measures which he was no longer allowed to control.

The resignation of Pitt was intensely unpopular. Bute was generally blamed for bringing it about, but quite unjustly. It was, as Dr von Ruville has pointed out, really due to the autocratic and domineering temper of Pitt, who resented the action of his colleagues in not meekly adopting his proposals. In any case, Bute became the object of popular hatred and hostility. The news that Pitt had accepted a peerage for his wife, and a pension of £3,000 a year for himself, caused a temporary reaction in public feeling. But it was charged against the King and Bute that they had pressed their favours on Pitt to discredit him in the popular eye. Pitt's admirers, however, were paying him but a poor compliment in representing him as falling into a trap laid by Bute. The King was very far from forcing honours on the retiring minister. George Grenville said that Pitt earnestly pressed for the peerage, and that the King was with difficulty induced to grant it. Pitt in a letter to Bute said that he should be "above all, doubly happy could he see those dearer to him than himself comprehended in His Majesty's monuments of royal approbation and goodness."

One of the most important steps to be taken by the young King was the selection of a consort. Bute sent Colonel David Graeme of Gorthy to visit the continental courts with the object of discovering a suitable queen for England. Colonel Graeme was a Scottish Jacobite who had learnt his profession in the Scottish Brigade in the service of Holland, and had been engaged in the Rising of 1745. Bute's employment of such a man was severely condemned, and cited as a proof of his dark designs on the constitution. David Hume said to Graeme, on his return from his embassy, "Colonel Graeme, I congratulate you on having exchanged the dangerous employment of making kings for the more lucrative province of making queens." As a result of the enquiries, the Princess Charlotte Sophia, youngest sister of Adolphus Frederick the Fourth, reigning Duke of Mecklenburg-Strelitz, was selected, and on the 8th September 1761 the marriage took place. The Queen was always grateful to Graeme for what he had done. She made him her Secretary, and in 1765 Comptroller of her household. She also bestowed on him one of the richest places in the gift of the Queen of England, the post of Master of St Catherine's Hospital.

An occurrence which took place soon after the marriage showed the feelings of the citizens of London with regard to recent events. On 9th November, "Lord Mayor's Day," the King, the Queen, Bute, and Pitt went to dine at the Guildhall. Bute was anxious about his reception. "My good Lord," he writes to Lord Melcombe, the umquhile Bubb Dodington, "my situation, at all times perilous, has become more so, for I am no stranger to the language held in this great city—'Our darling's resignation is owing to Lord Bute, who might have prevented it with the King, and he must answer for all the consequences.'" It was considered desirable to hire a number of prize-fighters for the protection of Bute's person. At Ludgate Hill his equipage was mistaken for that of Pitt, who was still intensely popular with the London mob, and loud applause greeted its passage through the streets. The error was discovered by the populace before the coach reached its destination. At St Paul's a voice exclaimed, " By God, this is not Pitt. This is Bute, and be damned to him." A terrible uproar followed the exclamation. Groans, hisses, yells, and shouts of " no Scotch rogues ! no Butes ! no Newcastle salmon ! Pitt for ever !" were heard, and it was with the utmost difficulty and danger that Bute reached the Guildhall. It was sometime before the unpopular minister was sufficiently composed to enable him to face the company which was assembled in the reception room. Pitt's equipage, which followed soon after Bute's, was received with tumultuous applause, while that of the King, which came last, was received with frigid silence.

In 1762 the King took the step which Pitt had desired him to do some little time before. He declared war against Spain. It has generally been regarded as a proof of Bute's incapacity that this step had now to be taken. It is said that Bute made a mistake in rejecting Pitt's proposals, and showed himself inferior in foresight to Pitt. Dr von Ruville has shown that this is a total misapprehension of the facts. Bute brought about the war intentionally, in opposition to Newcastle, the Prime Minister. The contest was by no means inevitable. In any case it proved a glorious one for Great Britain, largely, it is true, owing to the past efforts of Pitt. On 19th January 1762 Bute delivered his maiden speech, which proved a distinct success. " The few that dared to sneer at his theatric fustian," says Walpole, " did not find it quite so ridiculous as they wished." On 5th February 1762 he opposed the Duke of Bedford's motion for the withdrawal of British troops from Germany, and declared that a steady adherence to the German allies of England was necessary to bring about a speedy, honourable and permanent peace. His utterances are said to have been so manly and firm that the stocks actually rose a half per cent.

Since the retirement of Pitt, Bute had been practically the head of the Government. He desired now to be its real chief. The Duke of Newcastle, the Prime Minister, had lost all power, but clung to office with despicable tenacity. Nothing is so irritating as complacent incompetence, and George particularly disliked Newcastle, and treated him with habitual contempt. " The King," wrote the Prime Minister in November 1760, "has been remarkably cold and ungracious." When Newcastle strongly recommended a certain prelate for the Archbishopric of York, Bute asked him, " Why, if your Grace has so high an opinion of him, did you not promote him *when you had the power* ? " Endless slights were put upon him. Seven new peers were created without consulting him, and he not only submitted to the affront, but begged that Thomas Pelham, his cousin, might be added to the number. " It is extraordinary," remarked Walpole, " how many shocks will be endured by an old minister, or by an old mistress, before they can be shaken off." At last, on 26th May 1762, Newcastle resigned, and Bute took his place as head of the administration. The King offered Newcastle a large pension, but the offended nobleman declined it, saying that, if no longer able to serve his country, he would at least not be a burden to her. It is said that shortly after his retirement Bute sarcastically congratulated him on his release from the cares of office, which had been his delight. " Yes! yes! my Lord," said the Duke, " I am an old man, but yesterday was my birthday, and I remembered that it was just at my age that Cardinal Fleury *began* to be Prime Minister of France." So miserable did he feel out of office that a few weeks after he opened a negotiation for his return. He offered to renounce the Treasury and to content himself with the Privy Seal, an office without patronage, provided that, at the same time, the Earl of Hardwicke was made President of the Council. The Duke's borough interest was so powerful that Bute at first listened to the proposal, but, after consulting the Secretary to the Treasury, and examining the probable votes in both Houses, Newcastle was finally thrown aside. The disappointed old man went headlong into opposition, taking part with Pitt, and caballing in the city.

CHAPTER III

On 26th May 1762 the Earl of Bute became Prime Minister. Other changes were made in the Cabinet. Sir Francis Dashwood became Chancellor of the Exchequer, and George Grenville took the place of Bute as Secretary of State. Bute had been unpopular ever since the King's accession to the throne. He had been made the object of attack in lampoons and caricatures and pamphlets and even in sermons. Dr Dempster, to take a single instance, became a popular hero for preaching on 21st December 1760 before the King from the book of Esther, chap. v.—"Yet all this availeth me nothing, so long as I see Mordecai the Jew sitting at the King's gate." Caricatures of "Mordecai at the King's gate" were immediately after to be seen in all the print-shops. But, however unpopular Bute had been before, his accession to supreme power made him infinitely more hated.

"The new administration begins tempestuously," wrote Walpole on 20th June 1762. "My father was not more abused after twenty years than Lord Bute after twenty days. Weekly papers swarm and, like other swarms of insects, sting." The Whig aristocracy hated Bute as a Scottish upstart and an intruder into their charmed circle. Considering the work of governing the nation as their peculiar privilege, they resented the ambition of the Scottish favourite. The magnates lost no opportunity of inoculating the populace with their own ill-will. The dissenting ministers were particularly hostile. It is said that Bute had deprived them of an allowance of £2,000 a year, which they had hitherto received from Government, and Adam Smith believed this to be the reason of their virulence. The Prime Minister's supposed immoral connection with the Princess Dowager, his Scottish nationality, his influence with the King, were the subjects of the most malicious and vindictive lampoons and scurrilities.

"And oh! how the rabble would laugh and would hoot,
  Could they once set a-swinging this John, Earl of Bute,"

said Wilkes, expressing the popular sentiment. Even the Princes joined in the general hostility. When the King gave the Garter to his brother, Prince William Henry, and Bute, Prince Henry Frederick said, "I suppose Mr Mackenzie and I shall have the green ribands." Mackenzie was Bute's only brother. Some lines in the "New Foundling Hospital for Wit" commented on Bute's acceptance of the Garter—

"Oh Bute! if instead of contempt and of odium
  You wish to obtain universal eulogium,
  From your breast to your gullet transfer the blue string,
  Our hearts are all yours at the very first swing."

The popular emblems of the Princess Dowager and Bute were a petticoat and a *jack-boot*, a stupid pun on Bute's christian name and title. Those articles were paraded about the streets, followed by hooting crowds who ended by burning them with jeers and derisive shouts. An effigy of Bute hung on a gibbet at one of the principal gates of Exeter for a fortnight and no one dared to cut it down. The lampooners of Grub Street vied with one another in a general crusade against the minister. The most insulting caricatures were published.

One entitled "The Royal Dupe," pictures the young King as being lulled to sleep in his mother's lap, unconscious of the presence of Bute and Henry Fox, the former of whom is engaged in stealing his sceptre, and the latter in picking his pocket. In the western counties a figure of Bute, clad in tartan and decorated with the blue riband of the Garter, was paraded about, leading a donkey distinguished by the insignia of royalty. The King himself was personally insulted. One day when proceeding in his sedan-chair to visit his mother at Carlton House, a voice from the mob asked him whether "he was going to suck?" At the theatres every offensive expression that could be made applicable to Bute was cheered to the echo. When Mrs Pritchard, in Cibber's comedy of "The Careless Husband," spoke the words put into the mouth of Lady Easy—"Have a care, madam! an undeserving favourite has been the ruin of many a prince's empire"—the lines were received with rounds of applause. The alleged connection between Bute and the King's mother was the subject of endless scurrilities. The Princess herself was driven from the theatres by the filthy epithets hurled at her from "the gods." The story of Earl Mortimer, who was united by an illicit love to the mother of Edward III, and who, by her means, for a time governed the country and the king, became the favourite subject of the satirists. Among the papers left by Ben Jonson were the plot and the first scene of an intended play on the subject, and these were now republished with a dedication to Bute from the pen of Wilkes. Perhaps the grossest of all the caricatures was a frontispiece to one of the numbers of *Almon's Political Register*, in which Bute is represented as being secretly introduced into the bed-chamber of the Princess of Wales, the identity of which is rendered unmistakeable by a widow's lozenge, which, with the royal arms delineated upon it, is suspended over the head of the bed.

It has to be remembered that the mere name of Stuart was in itself a provocation to hostility. The Stuart princes had been exiled and deposed as the enemies of freedom. Here, it was said, was a Scottish nobleman bearing their name and descended from their race, trying to put into operation as prime minister the political principles, for which the Scottish dynasty had been banished. He was attacked as one who brought into English politics the despotic spirit of the Highland chief. His "close monasterial retirement" in Bute was supposed to have unfitted him "for anything but the tyrannic domain of a Highland clan." The popular belief in his attachment to the Stuarts was confirmed by such occurrences as the exclusion of the name of the Duke of Cumberland, so hateful to Scotsmen, from the liturgy. One issue of the *North Briton* in February 1763 consisted entirely of an imaginary letter supposed to be addressed to Bute by James the Third, the so-called Old Pretender. It begins "Dear Cousin," and ends, "given under our sign manual and privy signet of the Thistle, at our court at Rome, the second day of January, in the sixty-third of our reign. J. R., countersigned, James Murray." It congratulates Bute on his promotion of Jacobite interests. "Everything, through your benign influence, now wears the most pleasing aspect. Where you tread, the Thistle again rises under your feet. The sons of Scotland, and the friends of that great line of the Stuarts, no longer mourn." The letter praises Bute for providing for Jacobites and crushing the Whigs.

It exhorts him to continue to heap favours on the supporters of the Stuarts. It exhorts him to be cautious. "You have too soon dropt the masque." It says, "Do not aim too soon at the ministerial despotism we know you have in view. You may by too large strides miss your footing." The whole letter is a clever production, eminently calculated to damage Bute in the popular estimation.

To protect himself from attacks during his tenure of power, Bute had retained a body of political writers, who acted as his defenders and advocates. Hogarth had been created Sergeant-Painter to His Majesty's works soon after the King's accession, and did yeoman service for Bute. His support of the minister brought him into keen conflict with Wilkes and his friend Churchill the poet, who were trying to foment disaffection in the minds of the populace. Wilkes made a furious onslaught on Hogarth, whose friend and flatterer he had hitherto been. The best friends of Wilkes himself so disapproved of the attack that he was compelled to excuse himself by saying that he was drunk when he wrote it. Hogarth had a very ample revenge; he published the portrait of Wilkes, who was repulsively ugly and had a squint. "The renowned patriot's portrait," wrote Hogarth, "drawn like as I could as to features, and marked with some indications of his mind, fully answered my purpose. The ridiculous was apparent to every eye! A Brutus! a saviour of his country with such an aspect—was so arrant a farce, that, though it gave rise to much laughter in the lookers-on, galled both him and his adherents to the bone." Churchill, "Wilkes's Toad Echo," as the artist calls him, wrote an abusive *Epistle to Hogarth*. The artist resorted to the same method of revenge in his case as in that of Wilkes. "Having an old plate by me," he wrote, "with some parts ready, such as the background and a dog, I began to consider how I could turn so much work laid aside to some account, and so patched up a print of Master Churchill in the character of a bear." The print was published under the title of "The Bruiser," and represented Churchill as a bear, dressed in clerical garb, and holding a pot of porter in his right hand, and a club in his left. Hogarth obtained great satisfaction from the portraits of his two assailants. "The pleasure," he wrote, "and pecuniary advantage which I derived from these two engravings, together with occasionally riding on horse-back, restored me to as much health as can be expected at my time of life."

Tobias Smollett, the novelist, was another of Bute's advocates. This resolute and pugnacious Scot threw himself ardently into the battle on behalf of his highly-placed countryman. On 29th May 1762 he brought out *The Briton*, which fell upon Pitt with concentrated virulence. Smollett's weekly called forth *The North Briton* which first appeared on 5th June, and gave Smollett a Rowland for his Oliver. On 10th June Arthur Murphy, the biographer of Garrick, brought out *The Auditor* to second the efforts of *The Briton*. Pamphlets, skits and caricatures backed up the journals. Swarms of Grub Street scribblers hummed and buzzed like hornets. Among the obscurities who took part in the controversy was George Canning, the father of the statesman, who wrote a poetic *Epistle from William Lord Russell to William Lord Cavendish*, in which the doctrines of the Whigs of the Revolution were set forth for the benefit of the King and Bute. A crowd of writers were induced by places and pensions to support the ministry. It was said, though probably on no very sure authority, that more than £30,000 was expended on the press in the first two years of the reign. Dalrymple, who libelled Pitt in *Rodondo or the State Jugglers*, a production in rhyme (it cannot be called a poem), received the post of Attorney-General of Grenada. David Mallet or Malloch, the son of a small innkeeper at Crieff in Scotland, who had been for some time assistant-secretary to Frederick, Prince of Wales, wrote the tragedy of *Elvira* to serve Bute. It was acted at Drury Lane, and contained the words:

> "He holds a man who train'd a King to honour,
> A second only to the Prince he form'd."

Mallet received, in 1763, the post of Keeper of the Book of Entries for ships in the port of London. He was, like Dalrymple, a very poor writer, and Doctor Johnson said of him that he was the only Scot whom Scotsmen did not commend. It was not only obscurities who were employed to support the minister; baits were held out to the greater men. "Most of our best authors are wholly devoted to me," wrote Bute in February 1761, "and I have laid the foundation for gaining Robertson[1], by employing him for the King in writing the history of England; he must be pensioned." Even Doctor Johnson was granted a pension. Bute knew his man too well to attach any condition to his pension, but he no doubt hoped that Johnson would use his pen in his service.

Bute was conscious of the difficulty of the task that lay before him. Doubts as to his capacity for his high office forced themselves upon him. Eminent place is a severe task; it makes the great man greater than he is,

---

[1] The historian.

says La Bruyère ; the small man it makes less. Bute
admitted to Charles Yorke in September 1762 that he
was inexperienced. He told George Grenville that he
begged the King to allow him to retire, but that, when
he did so, the King would sit for hours afterwards with
his head reclining on his arm without speaking a word.
The objects of Bute's government were the establishment
of peace, the abandonment of continental connections,
the liberation of the Crown from the tyranny of great
families and party faction, and government without
bribery. In order to effect his objects, it was necessary
for him to obtain a majority in Parliament. Grenville,
who had taken Pitt's place as leader of the House of
Commons, was a man of firmness but deficient in tact.
An abler man was necessary to face the Whig opposition, which was certain to be intensely bitter. Henry
Fox, who was a Whig, was induced for financial considerations to undertake the leadership of the House.
He was a man of great ability, force, and daring, but
quite unscrupulous. It was his freedom from scruple
that qualified him for the work he had to do. " We
must call in bad men," said the King, " to govern bad
men." Grenville at first received the proposal to sur-
render the leadership with an "unspeakable astonishment
and with a rage not to be described," to quote Horace
Walpole. But in the end he was induced to consent.
Bute expected that the adhesion of Fox would bring
over some of the Whig leaders to support the administration, but the hope was not realised. Bute found himself
faced by a solid phalanx of opposition, and in the end,
in order to secure a majority, Fox had to resort to that
very bribery which the Tories had so strongly condemned.
Walpole relates that Fox, leaving the grandees to their

ill humour, directly attacked the separate members of the House of Commons. Gold was poured out like water. Some were influenced by their ambitions; others by their fears. Every kind of bait was held out to attract support. Placemen were told that their bread and butter depended on their votes. The work of bribery was carried on with so little decorum on the part of either buyer or seller that a shop was publicly opened at the Pay Office. There the members flocked and received the wages of their venality in bank bills, even to so low a sum as two hundred pounds. Mrs Warwick in *Diana of the Crossways* describes politics as "the school to mediocrity, to the covetously ambitious a sty,...Olympus to the genius." To Bute they were a school, in which he had much to learn. They were Olympus to Pitt, of whom Grattan justly said: "Great subjects, great empires, great characters, effulgent ideas, and classical illustrations formed the material of his speeches." To Fox politics were emphatically a sty. The letter in which Fox, writing to Horace Walpole, attempted to secure Walpole's nephew, Lord Orford, is worthy of quotation. He offered Lord Orford the Rangership of the London Parks at an income of more than £2,000 a year. "Such an income," wrote Fox, "might, if not prevent, at least procrastinate your nephew's ruin. I find nobody knows his Lordship's thoughts on the present state of politics. Now, are you willing, and are you the proper person, to tell Lord Orford that I will do my best to procure this employment for him, if I can soon learn that he desires it? If he does choose it, I doubt not of his, and his friend Boone's, hearty assistance; and I believe I shall see you, too, much oftener in the House of Commons. This is offering you a bribe, but 'tis such a one as one honest good-natured man may without offence offer to another." The money paid to Bute for His Majesty's Privy Purse and for the secret service gives some indication of Bute's subterranean expenditure. Between October 1760 and October 1761 £48,000 was paid for the Privy Purse and £95,000 for secret service; between October 1761 and October 1762 £48,000 went to the Privy Purse and £72,000 to secret service; and this was but a small portion of what was spent when Bute was in power.

CHAPTER IV

On 3rd November 1762 the preliminaries of a treaty of peace were signed at Fontainebleau by the Duke of Bedford and the Duc de Nivernais. The terms of the treaty were very unpopular and were much attacked. Wilkes described it as "the Peace of God, which passeth all understanding." It was declared by the Whigs that, if peace was to be made, much better terms should have been procured for England than were obtained. The navy of France had been nearly annihilated as early as 1759 by Sir Edward Hawke at Quiberon, and Spain could make little or no opposition to Britain on the ocean. The English were masters of Quebec, Montreal, and the whole of Canada, Cape Breton, Pondicherry, Goree, Belle Isle, the Havannah, a large part of Cuba, Manila, Martinique and Guadaloupe. The French, on the other hand, had taken nothing, which they had retained, except Minorca. By the treaty of peace France agreed to restore Minorca and to resign Canada, Nova Scotia, and Cape Breton, together with some territory, hitherto claimed as part of Louisiana. Spain ceded Florida and received back Havannah and Manila. Great Britain restored to France Belle Isle, Guadeloupe, Mariegalante, Martinique, and St Lucia, and retained Grenada, St Vincent, Dominica and Tobago. France was allowed a right of fishery in the gulf of St Lawrence and on the Newfoundland coast, and received the islands of St Pierre and Miquelon as shelters, covenanting not to fortify them. In Africa, England restored Goree to France and kept Senegal. In India, France abandoned her pretensions to conquests made since 1749, and received back the factories which she had at that date.

Bute was blamed for surrendering Guadaloupe and St Lucia to France. It must be remembered, however, that Pitt had offered to cede those islands in 1761, when Canada had been offered by France. Bute merely carried out what Chatham had been willing to do in 1761. The chief difference between the negotiations of Chatham in 1761 and those of Bute in 1762 was that Chatham refused to make any peace unless the King of Prussia concurred, while Bute was willing to treat without him. Bute was very much blamed for treating without the King of Prussia, and his enemies circulated a report that he had been actuated in making the treaty by a desire to revenge himself on Frederick for an epigram directed against the Scots. But the explanation of the different lines of action adopted by Chatham and Bute with reference to Frederick, is amply accounted for by the abject state of Frederick's fortunes in 1761 and his triumphant position in 1762. In the latter year his position was totally changed by the death of his enemy, Elizabeth of Russia, and the accession of Peter, who was a great admirer of Frederick. Bute had hoped that he would use this change of fortune to make peace, but it had only increased his eagerness to prosecute the war for Silesia. When he applied for the renewal of the English subsidy of £670,000, Bute informed him that it would only be granted on condition that he gave assurances that he was ready to make peace. Bute naturally

objected to paying out money for the aggrandisement of
Prussia. Frederick, however, refused to give the assurances required, and the British government not only
refused the subsidy, but made peace without Frederick.

In spite of the abuse showered upon the treaty of
peace there was much to be said for it. The war had
been enormously expensive. The drain of men and
money had been very great. The supplies granted in
1761 amounted to £19,616,119, while in that year about
180,000 British soldiers and sailors were in active service.
This was a very large number in proportion to the
population, and involved the necessity of offering high
bounties for enlistment. The national debt had increased
between 1755 and 1762, when the peace was made, by
sixty millions. It is not to be wondered at that the
King was eager to stop this enormous drain. The
treaty received the hearty approval of some of the most
eminent statesmen of the day. The veteran diplomatists,
Sir Joseph Yorke and Sir Andrew Mitchell, gave it their
entire approbation. The dying Carteret, Lord Granville,
who was the greatest authority on foreign politics in
England, said that it was the most honourable peace
this nation ever saw. It had the approval and support
of Lord Shelburne, whose modern biographer, Lord
Fitzmaurice, is also wholly in favour of it. The attacks
upon the peace were certainly not without precedent.
Lord Morley of Blackburn has pointed out in his
biography of Gladstone that, with the single exception
of the Peace of Paris in 1814, "every treaty concluded
at the termination of our great wars has been stigmatised
as humiliating and degrading, ignominious, hollow and
unsafe." Not only the Peace of Paris in 1763, but the
Peace of Utrecht in 1713, the Peace of Aix-la-Chapelle

in 1748, the Peace of Versailles in 1783, and the Peace of Amiens in 1801, were all so regarded.

One notable result of the treaty was, as has been stated, the cession of Canada to Great Britain. There were some who prophesied at the time that this event would prove disastrous to Great Britain. As far back as 1748 a Swedish traveller had predicted that the English colonies in America would in time form a separate state entirely independent of England. He stated that there was reason to regard the French in North America as the chief power which urged the colonies to submission. Later in the century Montcalm consoled himself for his defeat by the reflection that the loss of Canada would be of more service to his country than a victory. Wraxall also expresses the opinion that the expulsion of the French from Canada, and of the Spaniards from Florida, liberated the American colonies from all apprehension of foreign enemies, and laid the inevitable foundations of the rebellion, which effected their emancipation from Great Britain. He adds that this necessary result of the annexation of Canada was pointed out at the time by Dr Tucker, Dean of Gloucester, and others.

Parliament assembled on 25th November. Bute was hissed and pelted, and on his return had the glasses of his hackney chair broken. The preliminaries of peace were debated on 9th December. Bute made an able speech, greatly surprising his auditors, who had not regarded him as capable of such an effort. The Duke of Cumberland, who was strongly prejudiced against Bute, pronounced his speech to have been one of the finest he had ever heard in his life. Bute was seconded by the Earl of Halifax. The Earl of Hardwicke replied on the other side, but did not venture to divide the House. In the House of Commons the debate was dignified by the presence of Pitt, who had been quite unexpected. He was in a deplorable state of health, and made a most theatrical entry, supported by two attendants and clad in a suit of black velvet. Sitting while he spoke, he denounced the proposed treaty for three hours and forty minutes, but without avail. It was carried by three hundred and nineteen votes against sixty-five. In addressing the House of Lords, Bute expressed a desire that his having contributed to the cessation of the war should be engraved on his tomb. This hope gave rise to an epigram, which, at the time, was in everybody's mouth.

> "Say, when will England be from faction freed?
>   When will domestic quarrels cease?
>   Ne'er till that wished-for epitaph we read:
>   'Here lies the man that made the Peace.'"

It was charged against Bute that he made the treaty subservient to his own interest. It was said that he had made use of his ministerial position to acquire great wealth. His opponents pointed to his lavish expenditure. "Have we not seen him," wrote Anti-Sejanus in 1765, "for a time displaying his exorbitant treasures, in every kind of princely profusion? Has he not purchased estates, built and adorned villas, erected palaces, and furnished them with sumptuous magnificence?" When he went out of office he had scarcely completed a palatial house in Berkeley Square. His enemies declared that neither his own fortune nor the emoluments of office could have enabled him to construct that palatial residence. They did not scruple to say that he had either received gold from France, or had speculated in the funds, previously to the conclusion of the treaty. Dr Musgrave, an English physician practising in Paris, who published some tragedies of Euripides, boldly declared at the time that Lord Bute and the Princess Dowager received bribes from France for securing the peace. He was examined at the bar of the House of Commons in January 1770, but did not retract his accusation. The House, however, declared his assertions frivolous and unworthy of credit, and no credence need be given to the statement of this "idle busybody," as Brougham calls him. Accusations like those made against Bute have been only too common in the course of English history. Lord Clarendon, the Chancellor of Charles the First, built a magnificent house in London soon after the sale of Dunkirk to Louis the Fourteenth. The edifice was nicknamed "Dunkirk House," on the supposition that it had been erected with French gold. Lord Shelburne was attacked after the Treaty of 1783 on a similar charge.

It is in the highest degree improbable that the accusation of corruption against Bute was true. The inaccuracy of some of the statements of his opponents may be demonstrably proved. As late as 1789 Lord Camden asserted "that the rental of Lord Bute's paternal estate was only £1500 a year, and that he was sure he (Bute) got money for the peace of Paris." Yet among the papers of the family of Mure of Caldwell there is a rental of the Island of Bute for the years 1768 and 1769, which shows that the amount averaged for each of those years considerably over £3000 a year. And the rental must have increased between 1769, when the calculation was made, and 1789, when Lord Camden made his random statement. It is noteworthy that Burke in his *Thoughts on the Present Discontents* shows his disbelief in Bute's alleged poverty by describing him as "very ample in fortune."

As soon as the preliminaries of peace were signed, war to the death was commenced against the Whig aristocrats. The Duke of Devonshire, "the prince of the Whigs," as he was styled by the King's mother, resigned his post of Lord Chamberlain. On applying for admission to the Royal presence, after a short visit to the country, the King peremptorily declared, "tell him that I will not see him!" Six days afterwards the King with his own hand, struck his name out of the list of Privy Councillors. The courtiers insisted that the King was justified in his action. Not only, they said, had Devonshire habitually absented himself from the meetings of the Privy Council, but he was caballing with the Duke of Newcastle against the Government. He is said to have allowed his dislike of Bute to make him on one occasion disrespectful to the King. "The mob," writes Lady Temple to her husband at the end of December 1762, "have a good story of the Duke of Devonshire, that he went first to light the King, and the King followed, leaning upon Lord Bute's shoulder, upon which the Duke of Devonshire turned about, and desired to know which he was waiting upon." The Dukes of Newcastle and Grafton, and the Marquis of Rockingham were deprived of their Lord-Lieutenancies, and the same policy was extended to all classes. Even the humblest officials, who owed their places to Whig patronage, messengers and tax-gatherers, excise-men and custom-house officers, were dismissed. It was said, after the clearance of the Whigs, that Bute had dismissed everybody who owed his place to Whig influence except the King himself.

Fox's conduct in adopting the policy of proscription was severely condemned. "Fox," said the Duke of Cumberland, "has deceived me grossly, for I thought him good natured, but in all these transactions he has shown the bitterest revenge and inhumanity." It must be remembered, however, that the Whigs had been in power for nearly half a century. They had filled the public offices with men of their own faction, and, if the Tories were to have a chance at all, it was necessary that the vast body of government employés should be leavened by members of the party which followed Bute. A few Tories at the apex of a hierarchy of Whig officials were powerless, unless they could count upon some loyal supporters among their subordinates. While Fox was smiting the Whigs, as Samson smote the Philistines, his son, Charles James, was writing French verses at Eton, praising Bute, the "digne citoyen," and condemning Pitt, "un fourbe orateur," the idol and tyrant of a country, which the youthful poet blushed to call his own. Nine years after, when the youth had attained manhood, he said he did not believe his father had any hand in the proscriptions that were carried out at this time, but, if he had, it was right to break the power of the aristocracy that had governed in the name of the late King.

On 10th February 1763 the definitive treaty with France and Spain was signed at Paris. The passing of the Peace was a great triumph for the Court party. The Whig magnates were utterly routed, and the King did not hesitate to speak of himself as one providentially emancipated from an oppressive thraldom. The Princess

Dowager was heard to exclaim exultingly, "Now my son is King of England!" But successful as Bute had been in attaining his object his position was far from enviable. His difficulties were increased rather than diminished by recent events. The Whigs declared that the Peace was only the first step towards despotism, and the only return that Bute obtained for terminating a bloody and expensive war was increased abuse and unpopularity. The Whigs continued to raise so fierce an outcry against him that he dared not appear in the streets except in disguise by night, or unless protected by pugilists in the daytime. He was in constant danger from the mob. He went about the town, said Lord Chesterfield, timidly and disgracefully, attended at a small distance by a gang of bruisers, recruited from the scoundrels and ruffians that attended the Bear Gardens. The Whig magnates were as hostile as the populace, plotting and intriguing against the all-powerful favourite. It was Shakespeare's *King Henry VIII* over again. Bute was Wolsey, and the Whig nobles played the parts of Norfolk and Suffolk and Surrey in the drama.

> "We had need pray,
> And heartily, for our deliverance;
> Or this imperious man will work us all
> From princes into pages."

One of the most pressing duties of the Government was to provide for the pecuniary requirements of the nation. This was a task of exceptional difficulty. The cost of the war had been enormous, and fresh taxes were necessary. No one could have been less fitted for this post than Sir Francis Dashwood, the Chancellor of the Exchequer. He knew nothing of finance or commerce, and had hitherto been known chiefly for his scandalous immorality. One of the wits of the day said that he was a man to whom a sum of five figures was an impenetrable secret. There have been excellent Chancellors of the Exchequer who have known little about figures. It is said that Lord Randolph Churchill, when filling the same post as Sir Francis Dashwood, had to examine some figures in which decimals were used. He startled his subordinates by characteristically asking "what those d——d dots meant." But Dashwood, if weak in arithmetic, was far from having the ability of Randolph Churchill. He was himself perfectly conscious of his incompetence. " People," he said, " will point at me in the streets and cry, ' there goes the worst Chancellor of the Exchequer that ever appeared.'" His Budget was a remarkable production, and many of his expositions were received with shouts of derision. He laid a tax upon cider in the hands of the maker, which aroused intense opposition. Shelburne says that it was first proposed to put a tax on linen, but that Dashwood could not be made to understand it sufficiently to explain it to the House, and a tax on cider had to be substituted. The impost was debated on 28th March 1763, in the House of Lords, and Lord Hardwicke attacked it in a speech, which called forth a reply from Bute.

George Grenville defended Dashwood's Budget, and made the perfectly legitimate comment that it was the lavish extravagance with which the late war had been carried on that made additional taxation necessary. The Opposition, adopting the usual tactics, denounced the Budget, without suggesting sources from which money could be raised. Grenville, in the House of Commons, asked a question which has often been asked since, and which called forth one of Pitt's famous retorts. " I call upon the honourable gentlemen opposite to me," he repeated, in his usual querulous style, "to say *where* they would have a tax laid! I say, sir, let them tell me *where*! I repeat it, sir, I am entitled to say to them,— tell me where!" Pitt, fixing his eye contemptuously on Grenville, who was his brother-in-law, and mimicking his languid and monotonous tone of voice, convulsed the whole House with laughter by repeating the words of Howard's popular song, then familiar to all,

"Gentle shepherd, tell me where!"

He followed the sarcasm with a volume of invective which drove Grenville to fury, and then, with the most contemptuous look and manner, walked out of the House. Grenville was never afterwards able to get rid of the nick-name of "the gentle shepherd." But, after all, as Coningsby says in *Tancred*, "a majority is always better than the best repartee," and the tax on cider was carried by a large majority.

CHAPTER V

THE principal ground of attack upon Bute, or "the Thane," as he was nick-named, was his nationality. In order to understand why that was so, it is necessary to realise the feeling towards the Scots in the eighteenth century. The gap that divided the nations was still wide and deep. The intercourse between London and Edinburgh was so slight, that Sir Walter Scott, writing in 1818, relates that men then alive remembered an occasion when the mail from London arrived at the General Post Office in Scotland with only one letter. The old enmity engendered by centuries of warfare was slow in disappearing. The memory of the Highland invasion under Prince Charles Edward in 1746 long lingered among the English, who remembered with shame the panic which it had produced in London. The antipathy of the Whigs was increased by the Toryism, not to say Jacobitism, which was at that time a characteristic of Scottish writers. Hume's brilliant history, published in 1754 and 1756, was an elaborate apology for the conduct of the Stuarts. Smollett, whose writings were the delight of his day, was one of the most conspicuous advocates of the Court policy, and a keen supporter of Bute.

The tenacity of the Scots, their perseverance, their faculty for success, their imperviousness to rebuffs, their pedantry, their accent, all combined to make them disliked. The Londoner has ever amused himself with the national peculiarities of foreigners, and he loved to jeer at the characteristic qualities of the Caledonian. When Charles Macklin brought out his *Love à la Mode* in 1759 at Drury Lane Theatre, all the world flocked to laugh at his representation of Sir Archy MacSarcasm. So popular was the play that George the Second is said to have sent for the manuscript, and had it read to him. Macklin produced a still more popular caricature of the typical Scot in Sir Pertinax MacSycophant. The drama in which Sir Pertinax appears, *The Man of the World*, was not produced till some years after Bute's fall from power, but it is worth quoting here, because of the light it throws on the popular conception of the Scot in Bute's day. Horace Walpole said he had heard there was little merit in the play except the resemblance of Sir Pertinax to twenty thousand Scotsmen. In Act III., Scene I., Sir Pertinax acts the part of a Scottish Polonius, and explains to his son how he had attained his success.

Sir Pertinax.—...Why, you see, sir, I have acquired a noble fortune, a princely fortune, and how do you think I raised it?

Egerton.—Doubtless, sir, by your abilities.

Sir P.—Doubtless, sir, you are a blockhead. Nae, sir, I'll tell you how I raised it.—Sir, I raised it—by booing (bows very low)—booing, sir; I never could stand straight in the presence of a great mon, but always booed, and booed, and booed—as it were by instinct.

Sir Pertinax gives his son an account of his rise in the world. He started in the South in a beggarly clerkship in Sawney Gordon's counting-house in the city of London. Coming to the conclusion that he could improve his fortunes by matrimony, he married an antiquated but wealthy maiden, who was possessed of religious mania. Death soon relieved him of her presence, and he ran away with his second wife from a boarding-school. Her family interest took him into Parliament, where he made his fortune.

" Sir, I booed, and watched, and hearkened, and ran about, backwards and forwards, and dangled upon the then great mon, till I got intill the very bowels of his confidence ; and then, sir, I wriggled, and wrought, and wriggled, till I wriggled myself among the very thick of them. Ha! I got my snack of the clothing, the foraging, the contracts, the lottery tickets, and aw the political bonuses : till at length, sir, I became a much wealthier mon than one-half of the golden calves I had been so long a-booing to....But, Charles, ah ! while I was thus booing, and wriggling, and raising this princely fortune, ah ! I met with many heart-sores and disappointments fra the want of literature, eloquence, and other popular abeelities. Sir, guin I could but have spoken in the Hoose, I should have done the deed in half the time, but the instant I opened my mouth there, they aw fell a-laughing at me ; aw which deficiencies, sir, I detearmined, at any expense, to have supplied by the polished education of a son, who I hoped would one day raise the house of MacSycophant till the highest pitch of ministerial ambition. This, sir, is my plan ; I have done my part of it ; Nature has done hers ; you are popular, you are eloquent, aw parties like you and respect you, and now, sir, it only remains for you to be directed—completion follows."

When Bute attained the supreme power, the English saw the race of MacSarcasm and MacSycophant become omnipotent at Court, and were filled with fury. When they witnessed a Scottish Stuart all-powerful with the Monarch, when Scottish birth was a passport to success, and Scottish Jacobites were welcomed at St James's, they were full of spleen and spite. They pointed out

with indignation how many Scots held important posts.
Mansfield was Lord Chief Justice of England; Hay
Drummond was Archbishop of York; Sir Gilbert Elliot
and James Oswald were Lords of the Treasury; Sir
Andrew Mitchell was Ambassador at Berlin; Colonel
Graeme was the Queen's secretary; John Douglas, after-
wards Bishop, was Canon of Windsor; Lord Loudoun
commanded the British forces in Portugal; General
Murray had succeeded Wolfe after the taking of
Quebec; Lord Rollo, as second in command, was re-
ducing the Windward Islands; while a crowd of obscure
Scottish immigrants had obtained offices and pensions
paid for from the earnings of Englishmen.

The Scots were clannish and hung together. George
the Third said he had never known a Scotsman speak
ill of another, unless he had a motive for it. Doctor
Johnson once remarked to Boswell that no Scotsman
in London published a book or brought out a play but
five hundred of his countrymen were ready to applaud
him. Bute had the clannishness of his race. It was
noticed by the Opposition papers of the day that out of
sixteen names in one list of Gazette promotions there
were eleven Stuarts and four Mackenzies. This trait
helped to fan the flame of popular hatred. Caricatures
were published representing Bute as scourging Britannia
with thistles, and picturing the high roads to England
as crowded with ragged Scots.

> "But what comes here? Methinks I see
>   A *walking* University.
> See how they press to cross the Tweed,
>   And strain their limbs with eager speed;
> While Scotland, from her *fertile* shore,
>   Cries, 'On my sons, return no more.'

> Hither they haste with willing mind,
> Nor cast one longing look behind ;
> On ten-toe carriage, to salute
> The King and Queen, and Earl of Bute."

Buckingham Palace was nick-named Holyrood, because of the number of Scots who were said to resort to it. Wilkes and his associates rung the tocsin of national discord ; they poured out libations to the worst passions of the mob. Everything associated with Scotland was ridiculed and caricatured—the tartan and the kilt, the bagpipes and the blue bonnet, the haggis and the thistle. A typical cartoon of the day represents the Scots as dancing and rejoicing at a fire which is consuming John Bull's house. The centre of the picture is occupied by a great acting-barn, from the upper window of which Fox shews his cunning head, and points to the sign representing Dido and Æneas going into the cave, and announcing that the play of these two worthies is acted within. This is an allusion to the presumed intimacy between Bute and the Princess, who are exhibited as hero and heroine on the scaffolding in front.

Doggerel rhymes about the Scots were repeated with gusto by the mob.

> "Our manners now we all will change-a,
> Talk Erse, and get the Scottish mange-a,
>
>   *   *   *
>
> "A tartan each chield shall wear-a,
> With bonnets blue we'll deck our hair-a,
>
>   *   *   *
>
> "Then strut with Caledonian pride,
> Shakespeare and Milton fling aside ;
> On bagpipes play, and learn to sing all,
> Th' achievements of the mighty Fingal."

The poverty of Scotland was a perpetual source of

jest. Even the Prime Minister's island of Bute, which is about twelve miles long and five broad, did not escape ridicule. A ludicrous statement was made of the sum contributed by the island to the revenue, amounting to thirteen shillings and ninepence three farthings, subject to some deductions. The rapidity with which the Scots, once settled in England, emerged from poverty and attained a competence, was offensive to the Southron. They were denounced as leeches, sucking the blood of the poor Englishman, and as parasites weakening the nation among whom they had settled. John Wilkes contended that a Scot had no more right to preferment in England than a Hanoverian or a Hottentot. Horace Walpole gave the Scottish birth of Sir Gilbert Elliot as a conclusive reason why he should not lead the House of Commons, and the Duke of Bedford assigned the same reason as one of the objections to the appointment of Forrester to the Speakership. The old sarcasms about the alleged betrayal of Charles the First were revived and propagated. The King was warned that the Scots would act as treacherously towards him as they were stated to have acted towards his predecessor. The Duke of Cumberland, who had long been unpopular, partly because of his cruelty after Culloden, became the hero of the mob. His severities were now applauded, and his opposition to Bute was praised and extolled.

The most able of the assailants of Bute from the literary point of view was Charles Churchill, a profligate clergyman, the friend of the still more profligate Wilkes. Married at eighteen years of age within the rules of the Fleet prison, he took orders, and became curate and lecturer of St John's Church, Westminster. As might be gathered from the tenor of his career, the clerical profession was highly uncongenial, and he abandoned it for literature and vice. He assisted Wilkes by writing for the *North Briton*, and soon made himself conspicuous by his attacks upon the Scots, although it is said that his own blood was partly Scottish[1]. His satire on his northern fellow-subjects, entitled *The Prophecy of Famine*, was a huge success. It is said that he was highly pleased with the popularity of his poem, and dressed his youngest son in a Scottish plaid, like a Highlander, carrying him everywhere in that garb. The boy was once asked why he was clothed in such an unusual costume. He answered with great vivacity, " Sir, my father hates the Scotch, and does it to plague them." Churchill died in 1764, in his thirty-third year. Dr Johnson, who was himself satirised by the poet as *Pomposo*, called him a blockhead, but gave him the praise of fertility. " To be sure," said Johnson, " he is a tree that cannot produce good fruit; he only bears crabs. But, sir, a tree that produces a great many crabs is better than a tree which produces only a few."

Churchill delighted in presenting the Scots in the most ridiculous light.

"Jockey, whose manly high-boned cheeks to crown,
 With freckles spotted, flamed the golden down,
 With meikle art could on the bagpipes play
 E'en from the rising to the setting day ;
 Sawney as long without remorse could bawl
 Home's madrigals and ditties from Fingal ;
 Oft at his strains, all natural though rude,
 The Highland lass forgot her want of food,
 And whilst she scratch'd her lover into rest,
 Sunk pleased, though hungry, on her Sawney's breast."

[1] Thus he says in *The Prophecy of Famine*
" Madly I leagued against that sacred earth,
 Vile parricide ! which gave a parent birth."

He hated all Jacobites and supporters of the Stuart dynasty. He detested

> "Stuart's tyrant race
> or bastard or legitimate[1],"

and drew scathing pictures of the four Stuart Kings from James the First to James the Second in his poem *Gotham*. He regarded Bute as a foreigner, who brought discontent and misery into England.

> "When Bute with foreign hand,
> Grown wanton with ambition, scourged the land,
> When Scots, or slaves to Scotsmen, steer'd the helm ;
> When peace, inglorious peace, disgraced the realm,
> Distrust and general discontent prevailed."

The Scots, Churchill declared, were rebels at heart.

> "Those countrymen who, from the first,
> In tumults and rebellion nursed,
> Howe'er they wear the mask of art,
> Still love a Stuart in their heart."

Yet Englishmen preferred the Scots, Churchill complained.

> "For Englishmen alone have sense
> To give a stranger preference,
> Whilst modest merit of their own
> Is left in poverty to groan."

The Scots had always been a curse to England.

> "Scots, a fatal race,
> Whom God in wrath contrived to place,
> To scourge our crimes, and gall our pride,
> A constant thorn in England's side ;
> Whom first, our greatness to oppose,
> He in His vengeance mark'd for foes ;
> Then, more to serve His wrathful ends,
> And more to curse us, mark'd for friends."

[1] Bute was descended from an illegitimate son of King Robert the Second.

Churchill's principal attack on the Scots was made in *The Prophecy of Famine*, a poem of extraordinary vigour of thought and expression.

> "The Scots are poor, cries surly English pride,
> True is the charge, nor by themselves denied ;
> Are they not then in strictest reasons clear,
> Who wisely come to mend their fortunes here?
>
>   *   *   *
>
> "If they, directed by Paul's holy pen,
> Become discreetly all things to all men,
> That all men may become all things to them,
> Envy may hate, but justice can't condemn.
> 'Into our places, states, and beds they creep';
> They've sense to get what we want sense to keep."

Churchill draws a doleful picture of Scotland, which, in spite of its absurdity, is remarkably fine.

> "Far as the eye could reach, no tree was seen ;
> Earth clad in russet, scorn'd the lively green ;
> The plague of locusts they secure defy,
> For in three hours a grasshopper must die ;
> No living thing, whate'er its food, feasts there,
> But the cameleon, who can feast on air.
> No birds, except as birds of passage, flew ;
> No bee was known to hum, no dove to coo ;
> No streams, as amber smooth, as amber clear,
> Were seen to glide, or heard to warble here ;
> Rebellion's spring, which through the country ran,
> Furnish'd with bitter draughts, the steady clan ;
> No flowers embalm'd the air, but one white rose,
> Which on the Tenth of June[1] by instinct blows ;
> By instinct blows at morn, and when the shades
> Of drizzly eve prevail, by instinct fades."

Famine bids her countrymen leave this gloomy land, and depart to England, where

---

[1] The Jacobites wore a white rose on 10th June, the birthday of "James the Third."

> "For us, the earth shall bring forth her increase,
> For us, the flocks shall wear a golden fleece;
> Fat beeves shall yield us dainties not our own,
> And the grape bleed a nectar yet unknown."

Bute will make the way easy.

> "That son, of nature royal as his name,
> Is destined to redeem our race from shame;
> His boundless power, beyond example great,
> Shall make the rough way smooth, the crooked straight."

In the hatred of the Scots, professed by educated Englishmen, there was much affectation. Wilkes, who led the attack on the northern nation, could yet write, "I love the people of Scotland for their hospitality and friendship, as much as I admire them for their strong manly sense, erudition, and excellent taste. I never was happier than when in Scotland last." Unscrupulous politicians used the prejudices, which they did not share, for party purposes. Regardless of the evil effects of stirring up mutual antipathy in the two nations, they sought to make political capital out of the ravings of the mob. Fortunately there were some, who recognised the wickedness of such a line of conduct. Lord Chatham, to his great credit, would never join in the abuse of Scotland. He continually extolled the valour of the Highland regiments, and censured the conduct of those who were trying to create ill-feeling between the two sister countries. Even Lord Temple, although an intimate friend of Wilkes, strongly set his face against the so-called patriot's wholesale and brutal abuse of the Scots.

The feeling of enmity towards the Scots continued long after Bute's fall from power. It smouldered in the breasts of the ignorant until the end of the century.

It is said that George the Third himself constantly betrayed, as Lord Brougham says, "a very marked prejudice" against Scotsmen and Scottish politics. On one occasion, writing of Wedderburn to Lord North, he asked "Is Mr Attorney-General really running right? *I doubt all Scots*, and he has been getting everything he could." A similar hostility was shown by the Whig aristocracy. Brougham mentions it as a merit in Lord Holland that he did not share that feeling of contempt for Scotsmen that was held by other Whig leaders, Fox and General Fitzpatrick, Hare and Lord John Townshend. David Hume, philosopher though he was, complains bitterly of the hostility to his countrymen. "From what human considerations," he writes to Sir Gilbert Elliot, "can I prefer living in England than in foreign countries? Can you seriously talk of my continuing an Englishman? Am I, or are you, an Englishman? Do they not treat with derision our pretensions to that name, and with hatred our just pretensions to surpass and govern them?" In 1765 Sir Gilbert Elliot, a statesman of considerable eminence, made a vigorous protest in Parliament against the international jealousy, which had survived the Union, and declared that in his opinion Englishmen and Scots were one. If he himself had merit enough, he declared, he should pretend to any English place. The ill-feeling towards the Scots was as keen in the provinces as in London. Smollett, whose vivid pictures of contemporary English life may still be read with pleasure, made a tour in 1766, which he described under a thin disguise in *Humphrey Clinker*. He relates that he found all the inn windows from Doncaster northwards still scrawled with doggerel rhymes in abuse of the Scottish nation.

The memoirs of the latter half of the eighteenth century are rich in anecdotes at the expense of Scottish characteristics and peculiarities. Many an unhappy Scot had his pride wounded and his feelings hurt at London dinner tables, when the wine had loosened the tongues of the diners. Nothing delighted Johnson and his English friends more than to bait poor Boswell about the poverty of his countrymen. "Pray, Boswell," said Wilkes on one occasion, "how much may be got in a year by an advocate at the Scotch Bar?" "I believe two thousand pounds," replied Boswell. "How can it be possible to spend that money in Scotland?" asked Wilkes. "Why, sir," said Johnson, joining in the conversation, "the money may be spent in England; but there is a harder question. If one man in Scotland gets possession of two thousand pounds, what remains for all the rest of the nation?" "You know," added Wilkes, "in the last war, the immense booty which Thurot carried off by the complete plunder of seven isles. He re-embarked with three and sixpence." The magnetic attraction which the English capital exercised upon the more enterprising Scots and the large number of posts which they held in England were favourite subjects of jest. When at one of these pessimistic political conversations, so dear to Englishmen, it was lamented, "Poor old England is lost," Doctor Johnson replied, "Sir, it is not so much to be lamented that old England is lost, as that the Scotch have found it." When Doctor Ogilvie praised the noble wild prospects of Scotland, Dr Johnson remarked that the noblest prospect which a Scotchman ever sees is the high road that leads him to England. Wilkes told a friend at his board, who was praising his stewed pigeons, that he had tried to form a fine breed of them by getting them from France, but they always flew back. At last he got them from Scotland, and they never returned to their native land.

The extraordinary tenacity and perseverance of the Scots was one source of their unpopularity. One of the best examples of the successful Caledonian was Lord Glenbervie, who, beginning life as a surgeon, subsequently became a barrister and law reporter, and ultimately a peer and son-in-law to Lord North, the Prime Minister. Lord Ellenborough used to call Glenbervie "the Solicitor-General," because he always asked for everything that became vacant. Ellenborough used to swear that Glenbervie kept a Scotchman at half-a-crown a week, who was always on the look-out, and who sat up all night in order that he might call Glenbervie, if any one died in office. Lord Brougham relates that when the kingdom of Etruria was announced by Napoleon, and for some time no one was named, he and his friends were speculating who was to have it. "Don't you know?" said Ellenborough, "Glenbervie has asked for it and has great hopes." A Scot, who was out of employment, was supposed to be a rarity. "I am certainly the most unfortunate man in the world," wrote an English nobleman: "Two Scotsmen—the only two, I am persuaded, who are out of office and employment—have plundered the house in Hanover Square. I wish the administration had provided for them before. If I had been pillaged with the rest of the nation, I could have been content, but these private preferences are very unfair."

CHAPTER VI

THE facts related in the last chapter give some idea of the atmosphere in which Bute had to move when the Budget was passed in 1763. He had carried the Peace and he had carried the Budget. He was now triumphant, and England, as Walpole observed, was lying submissively prostrate before him. Suddenly on 8th April 1763 he startled every one by resigning. His enemies represented his step in the worst light.

> "With a sudden panic struck he fled,
>   Sneak'd out of power, and hid his miscreant head."

Bute told his friends that ill health and the unpopularity which he had been the means of entailing on the sovereign were the causes of his retirement. "Lord Bute," wrote Lord Barrington to Sir Andrew Mitchell, "resigned last Friday. He will have no office, and declares he will not be a minister behind the curtain, but give up business entirely. The reasons he gives for this step are that he finds the dislike taken to him has lessened the popularity which the King had and ought to have; that he hopes his retirement will make things quiet, and His Majesty's Government easy. He says that he unwillingly undertook the business of a minister on the King's absolute promise that he might retire when the Peace should be made." The truth was that Bute's position had become unendurable. The Duke of Newcastle wrote to Pitt, on the day after Bute's resignation, that the minister was thoroughly frightened from the universal resentment which he had drawn upon himself. The Whig peers were re-organising their forces with the assistance of Pitt. Their countenances, wrote Rigby to the Duke of Bedford, were quite cleared up when they had once put themselves under Pitt's management. Bute complained that he was inadequately supported by his own colleagues. " Single in a Cabinet of my own forming," he wrote to a friend, " no aid in the House of Lords to support me except two peers[1]; both the Secretaries of State silent, and the Lord Chief Justice, whom I brought myself into office, voting for me yet speaking against me—the ground I tread upon is so hollow that I am afraid not only of falling myself, but of involving my royal master in my ruin. It is time for me to retire."

Guicciardini finishes his history with the maxim, " Office makes the man." Bute had found the test too severe. It is possible that the King's disposition towards the minister may have been altering. Increased experience of men and things may have modified George's estimate of his early friend. It is asserted that Bute's influence over George had been for some time on the wane, and that the Earl, having secured a Parliamentary majority in favour of the Peace, the King had no great reluctance in accepting his resignation. The Duchess of Brunswick, the eldest sister of George the Third, told Lord Malmesbury years after that Bute expected the King to entreat him to remain in office, but that George had accepted the seals from the minister in silence.

---

[1] The Earl of Denbigh and the Earl of Pomfret.

There may have been another reason for Bute's retirement. By the death of his wife's father, Edward Wortley Montagu, he had succeeded to a noble fortune, and the emoluments of office were no longer a matter of importance to him. Horace Walpole stated the wealth of Montagu at one million, three hundred and fifty thousand pounds. Gray and Chesterfield put it at over half a million. Bute was a man of cultured and scholarly tastes, to whom the opportunities of study afforded by a retirement, free from pecuniary cares, would be far from unwelcome. His interest in natural science, his love of exploring

"All the wonders of a cockle shell,"

had been satirised by Churchill. To discuss art or literature with Dutens over a dish of tea was much more congenial to Bute than presiding at a cabinet council. Like many men who have been called in middle life to the work of the government without previous experience, he was wont to dwell on the miseries of his position and to profess a preference for an obscure life of peace. "One had better be a poor fisherman than meddle with the art of governing men," said Danton, and Bute is often heard expiating in a similar strain. "Why am I doomed," he wrote to Baron Mure in January 1759, "to climb ambition's steep and rocky height, who, early in life, had the meanest opinion of politicians—opinions that maturer age and dear bought experience too well confirm?"

When Bute retired, he named George Grenville as his successor. The new Prime Minister was not an attractive personality. He was able, courageous, hard-working, and upright. Like Mr Gladstone, he was a regular attendant at the church services, even when filling the highest offices. But he was narrow-minded, intensely conceited, and had no geniality or tact. He was a bad speaker. Walpole described him as a fatiguing orator and an indefatigable drudge. His nature was unforgiving and his manner ungracious. " I wish," said Sir Fletcher Norton to him in the House one day, " that the right honourable gentleman, instead of shaking his head, would shake an argument out of it." Grenville's sole delight in life was in the House of Commons. Lord Rosebery, writing of another lover of the House of Commons, says, " It was his mistress, his stud, his dice-box, his game-preserve; it was his ambition, his library, his creed." The same was true of Grenville. Once when he was taken ill and fainted in the House, George Selwyn, amidst loud cries from the members for ammonia and cold water, was overheard exclaiming, " Why don't you give him the Journals to smell to ? "

Grenville relied chiefly on the two Secretaries of State, Lord Egremont and Lord Halifax, for advice and assistance in carrying on the work of government, and the three were known as " the triumvirate." Lord Egremont was the brother of Grenville's wife and the son of Sir William Wyndham, who had been the champion of the Tories against Sir Robert Walpole. Chesterfield says he was proud, self-sufficient, and incapable. Lord Halifax, on the other hand, is described by the same writer, as possessed of parts, application, and personal disinterestedness. Whatever was the ability of the new ministers they soon found themselves in a sea of troubles. The cause of these troubles was the notorious John Wilkes. The King, in proroguing Parliament on 23rd April after Bute's resignation, spoke of the peace as honourable to the Crown and beneficial to the people. This statement produced an attack in Number XLV. of Wilkes's scurrilous paper, the *North Briton*, for which Grenville at once proceeded against the author. To detail the violent proceedings which followed that step is unnecessary ; they have been related a hundred times. Wilkes was imprisoned in the Tower, and became the hero of the mob. Popular feeling found vent in riots and disturbances, and the jackboot and the petticoat, the emblems of Bute and the Princess Dowager, were constantly in evidence. The fallen minister was the unhappy scapegoat on whom the blame for Grenville's action was laid. The unsatisfactory condition of affairs soon made the King dissatisfied with the ministry, and Grenville complained to His Majesty of his want of confidence. It was said that Bute had hoped to play the same part with Grenville as Pitt the younger in later years hoped to play with Addington. Grenville was to be the puppet, and Bute was to pull the strings. But Grenville, like Addington, refused to be a puppet, and Bute, having found him unmanageable, was said to have intrigued against him. No such explanation is necessary to explain the King's desire to get rid of Grenville. The Prime Minister bored and irritated his sovereign by his tiresome lectures and complaints, and George's dislike ultimately grew to such a pitch that he is said to have declared to Colonel Fitzroy that he would rather see the devil in his closet than Mr Grenville.

The sudden death of Lord Egremont gave an opportunity for a change in the ministry. The Duke of Newcastle was first sounded, but, in spite of his love of office, he refused to desert his friends. Bute, who had now attained to a better appreciation of the abilities and influence of Pitt, recommended the King to send for that great statesman. He himself called at Pitt's house in Jermyn Street on 25th August, 1763, and, having frankly acknowledged that the ministry could not go on, discussed the situation of affairs. On the next day, Friday, a message came from the King requiring Pitt's attendance. On Saturday Pitt went at noon-day through the Mall to the Queen's Palace. The great Commoner always had a keen eye to the effective and theatrical, and, desiring the world to realise his importance, had himself conveyed in his gout chair, the boot of which, as he himself said, made it as well known as if his name was written on it. The King and Pitt had a conversation on public affairs. As a result of the interview Pitt believed that he was to be Minister, and imparted his impression to the Whig leaders. He attended the Sovereign again on Monday, 29th August, but he was surprised to find a different atmosphere. He told the King that the affairs of the nation could not be carried on without the assistance of the great Revolution families. It was impossible, he said, to make a solid administration on any other basis. To re-establish the Whig oligarchy in power was exactly what the King was resolved not to do, and the negotiations were broken off. The Duke of Bedford said that the demands of Pitt's friend's, " the discontented great Lords," were so exorbitant, not to say insolent, that the King could not possibly grant them. " Should I consent to these demands of yours, Mr Pitt," said George the Third with considerable exaggeration, " there would be nothing left for me to do, but to take the Crown from my own head, and place it upon yours, and then patiently submit my head to the block." Walpole said the real stone of offence was Pitt's demand that his brother-in-law, Lord Temple, whom the King particularly disliked for his support of Wilkes, should have the Treasury.

The King was now in a humiliating position as regards Grenville. Grenville was furious against Bute, who had taken a prominent part in the negotiations with Pitt, and who, to use Lord Hardwicke's phrase, had "carried them to market in his pocket." The ministry insisted that Bute should retire from London to a place sufficiently distant to prevent his interference in the affairs of government. Egremont's post as Secretary of State had been taken by Lord Sandwich, a strange combination of ability and profligacy, "a second Anthony" as Chesterfield called him. Churchill describes Sandwich in scathing terms—

> "From his youth upwards to the present day,
>   When vices, more than years, have marked him gray,
>   When riotous excess, with wasteful hand,
>   Shakes life's frail glass, and hastes each ebbing sand,
>   Unmindful from what stock he drew his birth,
>   Untainted with one deed of real worth,
>   Lothario, holding honour at no price,
>   Folly to folly added, vice to vice,
>   Wrought sin with greediness, and sought for shame
>   With greater zeal than good men seek for fame."

Sandwich and Halifax goaded and urged Grenville on to the task of bullying the King. "My heart," wrote Charles Townshend, "bleeds for my sovereign, who is thus made the sport of wrestling factions." Bute agreed to leave London, but lingered in town. He was naturally unwilling to go into exile at the dictation of his former subordinates. His delay and his refusal to take up his residence on the continent gave Grenville an

excuse for depriving him of the office of Keeper of the
King's Privy Purse, which he had retained after his
retirement. At last Bute left for Luton, his seat in
Bedfordshire, and the ministry, relieved of his presence,
breathed more freely. There were many, however, who
still credited him with controlling affairs and influencing
the King. "You know," wrote Hardwicke, "Cardinal
Mazarin was twice exiled out of France, and governed
France as absolutely whilst he was absent as when he
was present."

The statement that Bute was still powerful is in
striking conflict with the truth as shadowed forth in
Bute's own utterances. Already he began to recognise
the ingratitude of his former friends, and the painfulness
of a fallen minister's position. "Sidonia has no friends,"
says the hero of Disraeli's *Coningsby*. "No wise man
has. What are friends? Traitors." The troops that
had bowed at Bute's levees and waited upon his smile,
had disappeared. He realised the truth of Shakespeare's
words—

> "Those you make friends,
> And give your hearts to, when they once perceive
> The least rub in your fortunes, fall away
> Like water from ye, never found again
> But where they mean to sink ye."

He moralises to his few faithful friends on the hollow
professions of the place-hunting world. In March 1764
he wrote to Baron Mure—"Few are the real friends
that fifty years of life has made; for within a twelve-
month I have seen so much that I blush at my former
credulity, and now know that the school of politics and
the possession of power is neither the school of friendship nor the earnest of affection. Attachment, gratitude,

love, and real respect, are too tender plants for ministerial
gardens. Attempt to raise them and they are either
chill'd on their first springing, or, if they once appear,
they fade with the very nourishment that is given them ;
and the unexperienced statesman fares exactly like the
woman who, fattening too much her hen, lost all her
eggs."

At the close of the session, 1763–4, Bute returned
to London, and the old jealousy was revived. It was
greatly increased in the following year, when the Regency
Bill was brought before Parliament. In January 1765,
the King fell ill, suffering from one of those fits of
mental aberration, which did so much to blight his life.
A Regency Bill was introduced on his recovery, and
Halifax and Sandwich, acting for the ministry, persuaded
the King that, if the Princess Dowager's name was
included as one of the persons who might be eligible
for the post of Regent, the Commons would demand its
omission, and the Princess would be exposed to public
insult. The object of this move was to prevent the
possibility of another Bute administration, if anything
should happen to the King. George the Third on
Halifax's representations, consented, though with great
distress of mind, that his mother's name should be left
out. When the Bill was introduced into the House of
Commons, the omission was at once observed, and a
large majority voted for its introduction. The King,
seeing the trick that had been played upon him, was
so indignant that he made a second effort to get rid of
the Grenville ministry. His anxiety for a new administration was increased by his intense personal aversion
to the Prime Minister. A persistent tradition avers
that Queen Victoria complained that Mr Gladstone

addressed her like a public meeting. It is not difficult to understand what the late Queen meant when she made that complaint, and, if Grenville had been her minister, she would probably have recognised in his manner a similarity to Mr Gladstone's. Grenville treated George like a schoolboy, boring and lecturing him *ad nauseam.* "When he has wearied me for two hours," said his Majesty on one occasion to Lord Bute, "he looks at his watch to see if he may not tire me for an hour more." Grenville himself noticed and constantly referred to the agitation displayed by the King during his declamations. His conceited dulness prevented him from grasping the cause of the King's annoyance. The Duke of Cumberland deeply sympathised with the unhappy position of his royal nephew. "There is no animal on the face of the earth," wrote Stuart Mackenzie, "that the Duke has a more thorough contempt for, or greater aversion to, than Grenville." The incompetence and incapability of the ministry added to the King's desire to part with them. They had displayed, to use his own words, "slackness, inability, precipitation, and neglect."

In May 1765 the King consulted the Duke of Cumberland about a change of ministry, and the Duke advised him to send for Pitt once more. Again, however, the negotiations fell through, chiefly through the hostility of Lord Temple. The ministry now refused to remain in office, unless the King pledged himself to fulfil certain sweeping conditions. He was to promise that Bute should never, directly or indirectly, publicly or privately, have anything to do with his business, nor give advice upon anything whatever. He was to dismiss Fox, now Lord Holland, from the paymastership. He was to turn Bute's brother, James Stuart Mackenzie, out of his place as Lord Privy Seal of Scotland. He was to give the post of commander-in-chief to the Marquis of Granby, who, famous as he was in his own time, is perhaps best remembered in these days as having given his name to the hostelry of Sam Weller's mother-in-law. He was to leave the appointment of Lord Lieutenant of Ireland in the hands of the ministry, which meant the dismissal of the Earl of Northumberland, the son-in-law of Bute.

The King was compelled to accept the terms of the ministry, which in his heart he now loathed and detested beyond words. He was greatly pained at having to dismiss Stuart Mackenzie. Stuart Mackenzie who was Bute's only brother, and who had taken the name of Mackenzie, on succeeding to the estates of his great-grandfather, Sir George Mackenzie, of Rosehaugh, had formerly been minister at the Court of Sardinia, and was a faithful and accomplished servant of the Crown. With the exception of his relationship to Bute, no fault could be found with this martyr to Grenville's prejudice. High-minded and capable, he enjoyed the cordial esteem of the King. Mackenzie had given up a lucrative appointment for that which he now held, and George the Third had promised that he should retain his new office for the rest of the reign. This promise had to be broken at the dictation of the prime minister. Mackenzie was regarded as the tool of his brother, a traitor in the camp, left to do Bute's bidding. His dismissal was part of the price which the King had to pay for enjoying the services of Grenville. George was greatly agitated at Grenville's demand, and strove in every manner possible to save his honour and his servant, but

Grenville was obdurate, and the King had to yield. The severity of the blow was greatly mitigated by George's kindness to Mackenzie, and the latter declared after the interview with his Sovereign, " If it were possible to love my excellent prince now, better than I ever did before, I should certainly do it." The King was greatly upset by Grenville's action. For some days he could eat little, and did not sleep above two hours at night, and the royal physicians had to be called in. The post of Privy Seal of Scotland was conferred upon Lord Lorne.

The arrangement patched up between the King and the ministry could only be short-lived. George had resolved in his own mind to get rid of the ministry at all costs. His position had reached the utmost limit of endurance. The tyranny of Grenville and his colleagues had become too great to be borne. " The King," swore Bedford's creature, Rigby, " shall not be allowed to appoint one of his own footmen." In June 1765 the Duke of Bedford addressed his sovereign in such terms that George himself said that if he had not broken out into a most profuse perspiration when the Duke had gone, his indignation would have suffocated him. " The King insulted and prisoner," wrote Walpole, "his mother stigmatised, his favourite persecuted—it is again a scene of Bohuns, Montforts and Plantagenets." But the Whig magnificoes who bullied the King had no weakling to deal with. No monarch more fully deserved the epithet *tenax propositi*. George continued his efforts to find a substitute for Grenville and on 10th July 1765 he had the satisfaction of dimissing the hated ministry.

CHAPTER VII

In July 1765, Charles, Marquis of Rockingham, became First Lord of the Treasury, in succession to Grenville. He was upright and wealthy, but of very moderate abilities. Even when Leader of the House of Lords, he could seldom be induced to address his peers. One night, after Lord Sandwich had been showering wit and raillery on the silent Minister, Lord Gower whispered to the speaker, " Sandwich, how could you worry the poor, dumb creature so?" The administration which was formed by Rockingham was composed of aged politicians, too old for efficiency, and young recruits without experience. " It is a heterogeneous jumble," said Lord Chesterfield, "of youth and caducity, which cannot be efficient." A witty remark which had been applied by Charles Townshend to a former adminis- tration was applied to the Rockingham Ministry :—" It is a mere lute-string administration," it was said. " It is pretty summer wear, but it will never stand the winter." The metaphor was singularly apt, and became generally popular.

> "A slight shot silk for summer wear,
> Just as our modern statesmen are,
> If rigid honesty permit
> That I for once purloin the wit
> Of him, who, were we all to steal,
> Is much too rich the theft to feel."

Bute had been credited, in spite of the King's denial, with instigating the dismissal of Grenville, and, before Rockingham and his friends would accept office, they resolved that absolute proof must be given to the world that neither directly nor indirectly should Lord Bute have any concern or influence in public affairs. They declared that, without this proof, it would be useless to attempt to form an administration. The Earl of Northumberland, Bute's son-in-law, was accordingly excluded from office, and Mackenzie, who had been dismissed at the instance of Grenville, was not restored to his former post. This action in taking measures to prevent the interference of Bute was probably unnecessary. It is asserted, with every likelihood of truth, that Bute had lost his influence some time before the final retirement of the Grenville Ministry. It is certain that after the accession of Rockingham Bute ceased to have any communication with the King on political matters. Bute himself gave his word of honour to the world, as published by his son, Lord Mountstuart, in 1778, that from the period when the Duke of Cumberland succeeded in organising the Rockingham Ministry in 1765, he had not only held no communication with the King, directly or indirectly, on any political subject, but that he had never once been in the King's presence, except at a Levee or a Drawing Room. He continued to visit the Princess Dowager regularly, but, when the King came to see his mother, he always retired by a back stair.

Lord Brougham says that George the Third took a strong dislike to Bute, and constantly betrayed a very marked prejudice against Scotsmen and Scottish politics. It is certain that Bute himself complained bitterly of the King's ingratitude. Wraxall relates an unsuccessful attempt that was made by Bute to recover his influence with the King. Despatches were often sent from the Secretary of State to George, when he was staying with his mother. When the green box containing the letters arrived, the King always withdrew into another room, in order to peruse them at leisure. On the arrival of the despatches on one occasion, Bute, as had been prearranged, immediately took up two candles, and proceeded before the King to the closet. He hoped to be invited to join the King in considering the papers, and thereby to get a footing in the Royal confidence. But George, seeing through the manœuvre, stopped when he came to the door of the room, took the candles out of Bute's hands, and retired alone. Bute, whose expectations were thus disappointed, returned to the company, and never repeated the experiment.

George the Third told his son, the Duke of York, that he never saw Bute after he left office except once, when, being with his mother in her garden at Kew, Bute came out of a summer-house, where he had been previously concealed. The King added that he effectually showed his displeasure at the intrusion of his former favourite. Lord Brougham tells a similar story, which is probably a variation of that just related. The Princess Amelia, the aunt of the King, invited Bute to her villa at Gunnersbury, near Brentford, on a day when George was to visit her. The former Minister was walking in the garden when she took her nephew downstairs to view it, saying there was no one there but an old friend of his, whom he had not seen for some years. George had no time to ask who it might be, before he was led into the garden, and there he saw Bute walking up an alley. The King, says Brougham, instantly turned back to avoid him, reproved his aunt sharply, and declared that, if she ever repeated such experiments, she had seen him for the last time in her house.

The Rockingham Ministry was not long in power before it got into difficulties. There is reason to believe that, in their trouble, they applied to the King to solicit Bute's support in Parliament. The King said he knew nothing of what Bute was doing, and must decline sending for him. Not only the Ministry, but even the Opposition endeavoured to secure the assistance of the once-powerful favourite. George Grenville and Lord Temple, his brother, with the Duke of Bedford, approached Bute, and an interview was arranged between them at Lord Eglinton's house. At this interview Lord Temple did not appear, and it has been suggested that he had discovered, by means of the spies whom he was in the habit of using to watch Bute's movements, that the former Minister had become completely estranged from the King, and had lost all his influence. On 12th February 1766, Bute, Grenville, and Bedford met as arranged. "The Favourite," wrote Walpole, "had the triumph of beholding the Duke of Bedford and George Grenville prostrate before him; suing for pardon, reconciliation, and support. After enjoying this spectacle of their humiliation for some minutes, the lofty Earl, scarce deigning to bestow upon them half-a-score of monosyllables, still refused to enter into connexion with them." In granting the interview, Bute, probably did so merely to enjoy a triumph over his former enemies. He declared he was not to blame for their disappointment. The meeting, as he plainly told them, was not of his seeking, and, if Lord Eglinton had led them to believe so, it must have been either ignorantly, or from good intentions on the part of that nobleman. As regarded His Majesty, Bute declared he never saw him, and knew nothing of his opinions. At parting, the Duke of Bedford condescended to express a hope that their meeting would be kept a secret. "There is nothing of which I am ashamed," was Bute's reply.

In spite of the most positive denials of both the King and Bute, it was long believed that Bute continued to influence the counsels of his Sovereign.

> "That haughty, timid, treacherous thing,
> Who fears a shadow, yet who rules a King."

He was accused of setting the Sovereign against his Ministers, of pouring his "leprous distilment" in the Royal ear. When Cumberland died in September 1765, he was regretted as the most powerful opponent of the influence of "the Thane," and prints and caricatures represented Bute as dancing over the Duke's tomb, and rejoicing in the recovery of power. When the Rockingham Ministry fell in August 1766, Bute was at once charged with bringing that event about, although he wrote at the time that, save from the newspapers, he knew as little of the affairs of England as of those of Persia. In Walpole's opinion, he was still "the idol that keeps behind the veil of the sanctuary." Absurd stories were told of his having been seen lurking in country roads round about Kew, going to or returning from secret interviews with the King. Nor was the belief in Bute's influence confined to Great Britain. In 1765 the people of Quebec complained bitterly of James Murray, their Governor, and they approached Lord Bute, amongst others, with a view to the redress of their grievances. They applied to Bute from the belief that Murray was patronised and protected by him. In December of the same year the people of New York, who were in a ferment over the Stamp question, blamed Bute, among others, for their troubles. The Society of the Sons of Liberty carried the effigies of Lord Bute, Grenville, and Governor Murray in a procession through the streets, and afterwards marched to the fields, where they burnt them.

Pitt lent further countenance to the delusion about Bute's influence, when he formed his administration in succession to Rockingham. He had the courage to remedy the injustice done to Stuart Mackenzie, Bute's brother, and re-appointed him to his former office of Lord Privy Seal of Scotland. The reinstatement of Mackenzie, coupled with Pitt's acceptance of a peerage, revived the legend of Bute's influence in full force, and Pitt, of all persons in the world, was attacked as the nominee of the fallen Minister. Thomas Hollis, the philanthropist and republican, who had been a great admirer of Chatham, " bemoans the recent unparalleled prostitution and apostasy of the once magnanimous and almost divine[1] * * * who is now fatally lost in parchment and Buteism." Four months after he speaks of Chatham as "Lieutenant Turnover, acting as commander-in-chief, at this present; by permission of Whiterose[2], the favourite, who would be thought retired."

Bute was overwhelmed with obloquy for his supposed interference with the new Government. In a letter of 24th June 1767, written by Anti-Sejanus, and ascribed (probably erroneously) to Junius, it is said, " To create

[1] Chatham.

[2] Bute is so called in reference to his supposed Jacobite propensities.

or foment confusion, to sacrifice the honour of a king, or to destroy the happiness of a nation, requires no talent but a natural *itch* for doing mischief. We have seen it performed for years successively, with a wantonness of triumph, by a man who had neither abilities nor personal interests, nor even common personal courage. It has been possible for a notorious coward, skulking under a petticoat, to make a great nation the prey of his avarice and ambition." Bute was constantly compared to Sejanus, the despotic Minister of Tiberius, and the Princess Dowager was likened to Livia, the mother of the Emperor, a woman, says Tacitus, "*muliebri impotentia*, raging with all the impotence of female ambition." In 1767 there began to be great talk among doctors of the virtues of the *carduus benedictus*, or blessed thistle, as a universal remedy, and the plant, worshipped by the quacks, was soon adopted as an emblem of Bute. Bute was said to be aiming at the recovery of power on Chatham's resignation in 1768. The shadow of Bute troubled the populace as persistently as King Charles' head troubled David Copperfield's friend. A print, dated 1770, suggested a design for a new crown piece, and gave the converse and reverse of the proposed coin. On the latter, Britannia is represented in bonds, while Bute tramples on her shield, and the sun is shining brightly upon a thistle. An inscription round the edge runs, "*Le soleil d'Ecosse aux Angloises feroce*,—the sun of Scotland fierce to the English." The other side of the suggested coin represents the head of Bute between those of the King and the Princess Dowager, with the inscription, "*Tria juncta in uno*,—three joined in one." Ten years after his accession the King was still supposed to be under the control of the jack-boot and petticoat.

Nothing could stop the persistent misrepresentation that dogged the footsteps of Bute. It was in vain he proved the impossibility of his influencing the King. "Cut scandal's head off, still the tongue is wagging," said Garrick in his prologue to Sheridan's *School for Scandal.* No assertion, however positive, could prevent Bute from being calumniated and slandered by those who should have known better, and the populace, like village curs, barked when their fellows did. Dutens says that long after his fall Bute received both letters of solicitation and anonymous communications, which he would give to Dutens to read, and then throw into the fire. Like many reserved and silent men, he was very sensitive, and the constant attacks which were made upon him grieved him deeply. In July 1768, when about to leave England, he wrote to John Home, author of *Douglas,* " I will apprise you how to direct to me, as I shall not leave my name behind me for these vipers to spread their venom on. For, believe me, whatever advantage to my health this odious journey may be of, I know too well the turn of faction to suppose my absence is to diminish the violence I have for so many years experienced....I have tried philosophy in vain, my dear Home : I cannot acquire callosity ; and were it not for something still nearer to me—still more deeply interesting—I would prefer common necessaries in Bute, France, Italy, nay Holland, to fifty thousand pounds a year within the atmosphere of this vile place." It cannot be said that Bute bore his troubles like a Stoic. He did not enjoy good health, and his daughter, Lady Louisa Stuart, describes him in later life as frequently ailing, and taking "loads of physic." The grief to which he gives vent in the pathetic letter, just quoted, added to bad health and family afflictions, made him a truly miserable man. To receive the blows of adversity with dignity and equanimity is to conquer adversity. " He that tholis overcummis," ran the motto above the door of an ancient house that used to stand in the West Bow of Edinburgh. He that endures overcomes. But the slings and arrows of outrageous fortune wounded Bute to the heart. Restless and unhappy, he wandered about Italy, hiding his personality under the incognito of " Sir John Stuart." Writing to Home from Venice in October 1770 he says, " Near three months of this envenomed Sirocco has lain heavily on me, and I am grown such a stripling, or rather a withered old man, that I now appear thin in white clothes that I looked Herculean in when I was twenty. I hope I may get better, if permitted to enjoy that peace, that liberty which is the birthright of the meanest Briton, but which has been long denied me." Strangely enough, the legend of his great influence with the King persistently followed him, even in France. There, however, the belief in that influence had pleasanter consequences than in England. During his stay at Barèges, where he went to drink the mineral waters, the French Court ordered him the same guard at his lodgings as if he had been a Prince of the Blood.

It has been said that no amount of protests on Bute's part could destroy the conviction that he ruled the King. " When that noxious planet approaches England," wrote Junius of Bute in 1771, " he never fails to bring plague and pestilence along with him." Ten years after George came to the Throne Chatham was still harping on the old theme. Bute was Mazarin over again, and the Princess was Anne of Austria. " That favourite," said Chatham, "is at the present moment abroad, yet his influence, by his confidential agents, is as powerful as if he were at home. Who does not know the Mazarinade of France?—that Mazarin absent was Mazarin still? And what is there, I would ask, to distinguish the two cases?" In 1771, during the dispute between the House of Commons and the printers as to the publication of the Parliamentary debates, the effigies of Bute and the Princess Dowager were carried in carts to Tower Hill, where they were beheaded by chimney-sweepers before a large crowd, and committed to the flames.

Bute's old colleague, Lord Holland, who had done the dirty work in carrying the Peace of Paris, and who was anxious to be made an Earl, appealed to Bute for assistance. "Do you remember," he asked, "you who never deceived me, when you told me, if I asked anything for my children, I should see the esteem the King had for me? I see no signs of it." Bute's answer was a confession of powerlessness. "The very few opportunities I have had for many years," he said, "of being of the least service to any person are now at an end. The sad event of this fatal year[1] has left me without a single friend near the Royal person, and I have taken the only part suited to my way of thinking—that of retiring from the world before it retires from me." He makes a similar admission of his utter lack of influence in March 1773. "Think, my friend," he wrote to Home, "of my son Charles being refused everything I asked! I have not had interest to get him a Company, while every alderman of a petty corporation meets with certain

[1] The death of the Princess Dowager in February, 1772.

success. I am now in treaty, under Lord Townshend's wing, for dragoons in Ireland. If I don't succeed, I will certainly offer him to the Emperor." To be entirely powerless was galling enough; to be abused at the same time as a modern Sejanus was indeed a hard fate. In November 1774, Lord North had the good sense to admit that Bute's influence with Royalty was a fable. Bute was elected a Representative Peer for Scotland, and Lord North said, "A Dowager First Lord of the Treasury has a claim to this distinction, and we do not now want a *coup d'état* to persuade the most ordinary newspaper politician that Lord Bute is nothing more."

But, if Lord North was willing to admit that Bute had no influence with the King, it was not admitted by others. Early in 1778 Sir James Wright and Dr Addington, Chatham's physician and father of the first Lord Sidmouth, made an unsuccessful attempt to bring about an alliance between Bute and Chatham. Bute on this, as on so many other occasions, unequivocally denied his influence with the King, and declared that he had no wish to take any part in public affairs. When the "No-Popery" cry was raised in 1780, the old legend that Bute was a Jacobite was again revived, and it was declared that he was aiming at the aggrandisement of the Stuart dynasty. A caricature represented George the Third as sleeping, while some Scotsmen lifted his crown. Bute, in plaid and bonnet, asks another in wig and ermine, "What shall be done with it?" The reply is, "Wear it yoursel', my laird." But another exclaims, "No, troth, I'se carry it to Charley, and he'll not part with it again."

In 1780 Bute, being then sixty-seven years old, retired from Parliament at the dissolution, on the score of old age. But even two years after, in 1782, on the formation of the second Rockingham administration, Horace Walpole wrote, "It was thought the King saw Lord Bute on that occasion; for others he certainly sent." Bute spent the last six or seven years of his life chiefly at Christchurch, Hampshire, where he had a villa on the edge of the cliff, over-looking the Needles and the Isle of Wight. He had little taste for cheerful society, and it is said that his principal occupation there was listening to the melancholy roar of the waves. It may be that the plaintive voice of the ocean brought consolation to a spirit broken by what he believed to be the unkindness and ingratitude of mankind. If he ever read Shakespeare, he might have pondered the magnificent words, which are put into the mouth of Wolsey :—

> "This is the state of man; to-day he puts forth
> The tender leaves of hope, to-morrow blossoms,
> And bears his blushing honours thick upon him;
> The third day comes a frost; a killing frost;
> And—when he thinks, good easy man, full surely
> His greatness is a-ripening,—nips his root,
> And then he falls as I do."

In November 1790 Bute met with a serious accident; he fell twenty-eight feet over a cliff near his house. He did not appear to have suffered any injury except a sprained ankle, and Horace Walpole spoke of him as recovering well for a man of seventy-seven years of age. But the shock told on him none the less, and on 10th March 1792 he died at the age of seventy-eight in his house in South Audley Street, Grosvenor Square. He was buried at Rothesay, in his own ancestral island in Scotland.

CHAPTER VIII

THE question of Bute's character is an interesting one. The most contradictory assertions and statements are found in contemporary literature. He had his admiring eulogists. His friend and frequent guest, M. Dutens, speaks of him in terms of warm admiration. Lady Hervey wrote in December 1760, "So much I know of him, though not personally acquainted with him, that he has always been a good husband, an excellent father, a man of truth and sentiments above the common run of men. They say he is proud. I know not. Perhaps he is. But it is like the pride they also accuse Mr Pitt of, which will always keep them from little, false, mean, frivolous ways; and such pride may all that I love or interest myself for, ever have."

The chief objection to Bute was undoubtedly his Scottish nationality. Lord Morley has justly said that he fell less from disapproval of his policy than from rude prejudice against his country. Many testimonies to this fact might easily be adduced. "Lord Bute," said Bishop Warburton, "is a very unfit man to be Prime Minister of England. First, he is a Scotchman; secondly, he is the king's friend; and thirdly, he is an honest man." Lord Chesterfield is equally explicit. "The great cry against Lord Bute," he wrote, "was on account of his being a Scotchman; the only fault which he could not possibly correct." In the eighteenth century the English people had not acquired that tolerance of foreigners and aliens that they exhibit to-day. The motto of Wilkes's magazine, *The North Briton*, was Virgil's words, " nostris illuserit advena regnis." Bute was the *advena*, the stranger, the alien. Sichel in his book on Beaconsfield, who was also attacked as an alien, hazards the opinion that in the eighteenth century a Scotchman like Bute was looked upon much as an Italian Jew was at the beginning of the nineteenth century.

In after years, when prejudice had died down and old bitterness was forgotten, men realised that historical justice required a considerable mitigation of the contemporary criticism of Bute. Burke, although opposed to Bute, truly said that much the greater part of the topics, which had been used to blacken him, were either unjust or frivolous. No one was more severe in his criticisms than Horace Walpole; yet in later life Walpole seems to have materially changed his opinions in regard to the somewhat harsh judgment which he had formed of Bute's abilities and motives. " Lord Bute," he said, "was my schoolfellow. He was a man of taste and science ; and I do believe his intentions were good. He wished to blend and unite all parties. The Tories were willing to come in for a share of power, after having been so long excluded ; but the Whigs were not willing to grant that share. Power is an intoxicating draught. The more a man has the more he desires."

More than one distinguished historian of modern times has refused to accept the contemporary verdict on Bute. Dr Von Ruville, whose opinion is of the highest value, thinks that the unfavourable judgment passed upon Bute by history is quite without justification. He considers that he had no capacity for statesmanship, though his political powers were by no means despicable. But he entirely endorses Macaulay's statement that " he was a man of undoubted honour." " His relations with the King," says Von Ruville, "were those of honesty and devoted friendship, of a strength rarely found in England. It was a friendship characterised by the fidelity of the Highlander. English nobles generally served the King in the hope of securing wealth or power, and occasionally out of pure patriotism, but Bute served him for reasons of personal devotion and affection. He was not primarily anxious to increase the power of the state or of the monarchy; this was only a means to an end, as his object was to be of use to his master, George III, and to make his reign as happy as possible, a desire that is repeatedly obvious in his private correspondence. Bute was no bad judge of the kind of man needed for the King's service, and had a fine instinct for all who could contribute to strengthen his master's position; hence it may be said that he was exceptionally suited for the post of confidential adviser." Bute, it has been said, wanted to protect George III from Pitt in much the same way as Prince Albert sought to protect Queen Victoria from Palmerston.

Mr Beckles Willson, the Canadian writer, is equally favourable in his description of Bute. " Looking back now," he says in his work on George III, " upon the politicians of that time, Bute seems to us almost, if not quite, the worthiest. He was well read, a clear, sane thinker, uncorruptible; a real patriot. He was no master of those demagogic words in which Pitt and Wilkes excel; neither his tongue nor his pen could scatter vitriol, and he suffered under a disadvantage which the statesmen of our day have overcome with triumphant success—the disadvantage of being a Scotsman."

Mr D. A. Winstanley, of Trinity College, Cambridge, in his able book on *Personal and Party Government*, has given an excellent account of Bute's ministerial career. He acquits him of the charges of baseness and selfishness. "His talents," says Mr Winstanley, "did not lie in the direction of public life, and, realising his own limitations, he preferred to be the prompter in the wings rather than the actor on the stage. Bute was not of the order of royal favourites, who exploit the crown to promote their own advancement. On the contrary it seems that not selfish ambition but genuine affection for the King's person led him to take his place in the political arena ; and, though he may have been unwise, he was not base. He displayed an unfeigned reluctance to assume the cares of administration, but he had to struggle against a will stronger than his own. His pupil and master had determined that he should have high office in the ministry, and that men should learn that there were other avenues to greatness than the favour of the Whig party."

Mr Winstanley lays emphasis on the fact that Bute was extremely unwilling to take office. It was the King who pressed him into it. "The promotion of Bute," says Mr Winstanley, "was to be the outward and visible sign of the restoration of the royal authority." He quotes Bute's letter of 24th March 1761, to the King. "I take the office," wrote Bute, "that of all others my mind has the most repugnance to, and I am torn from one that I have reason to dote on. Each fond wish of my heart crys out against this important change, but duty and gratitude condemns one to the trial. I make it then, but not without violent emotions and unpleasant forebodings."

Lord Rosebery takes a view of Bute which is at variance with that of the historians quoted above. He thinks that it is probable that George the Third never liked Bute, and that Bute's direct influence over him has been greatly exaggerated. In a communication which he has been good enough to make to the present writer, Lord Rosebery says that in his opinion the regard for Bute was chiefly on the part of the mother of George the Third, and that after a time the King discovered what were presumed to be his mother's relations with Bute, and regarded him with aversion. Lord Rosebery thinks that the influence of Bute was solely due to the Princess Dowager of Wales. The opinion of Lord Rosebery on any point of eighteenth century history is, of course, extremely valuable, but in this matter the view of most modern historians, as will be seen from what has been said above, differs from that of Lord Rosebery.

The charges of immorality against Bute and the Princess were in the highest degree improbable. That the silent, middle-aged Scotsman, with his large family, should have played the part of "Lothario" to "the grave, lean, demure, elderly woman," as Thackeray calls her, with her eight children, seems absurd and impossible. It was an age of unscrupulous abuse, and, in times of popular passion, the cleanest characters were bespattered with mud. Every one knows, to take a single instance, how the early career of Burke was hampered by the ridiculous accusations of Jacobitism and Jesuitism to which he was subjected. Wilkes, to his friends, did not hesitate to declare his absolute disbelief in the reports about Bute and the Princess, although he did not fail to insinuate them in the *North Briton*. Bute unwisely surrounded his visits to Carlton House with an air of mystery, which awakened suspicion. He invariably went to see the Princess in the evening, generally using the sedan chairs and the chairmen of Miss Vansittart, a lady who held a distinguished place in the family of the Princess. The curtains were always closely drawn— a precaution which may have been due to fear of insult, but was set down to other causes. Horace Walpole said that the eagerness of the pages of the backstairs to let the Princess know whenever Lord Bute arrived, and some other symptoms, contributed to dispel the ideas that had been conceived of the rigour of her widowhood. " I am as much convinced," he wrote, " of an amorous connection between Bute and the Princess Dowager as if I had seen them together." That suspicions of a connection between Bute and the Princess were current even in the lifetime of Prince Frederick is shown by the well-known retort addressed to her by her maid of honour, the notorious Miss Chudleigh, who was afterwards to figure in the law courts as Duchess of Kingston. Miss Chudleigh appeared in a half-nude state as Iphigenia at a masked ball at Somerset House, and the Princess pointedly rebuked her immodesty by throwing a veil over her person. "Votre altesse royale," said the impertinent maid of honour, "sait que chacune a son But."

The scandalous rumours were not justified by any known facts. The popular belief was founded on surmise and what Lord Chesterfield called " mere conjectures." The scandal about the Princess Augusta recalls the scandal about another royal lady, Queen Caroline, the wife of George the Fourth. A large section of the English people was firmly convinced that she was a woman of dissolute character. Even her own counsel, Denman, appears to have doubted her innocence. Yet few competent judges, examining the evidence now, when all prejudice and feeling have disappeared, would hesitate for a moment to pronounce her guiltless of the charges brought against her. Nothing is so persistent and so readily believed as scandal, however absurd, about persons in high station.

> "Destroy his fib, or sophistry in vain;
> The creature's at his dirty work again."

When this fact is remembered, it is well to be very wary in accepting the scurrilous reports about Bute and the Princess Dowager.

Whether or not there was an "amorous connection" between the two, they were certainly bound together by a strong bond of friendship. Amidst all the obloquy and abuse that were heaped upon the minister's head, the Princess stood his loyal and devoted friend. Her support and sympathy never failed amidst all his trials. She was the Egeria to whose counsel and advice he ever resorted. Her attachment consoled him, when others were falling away. When the Princess died in 1772 of a throat complaint, Bute felt his loss very keenly. He placed a pathetic inscription on a pillar in Luton Park, evidencing his devotion to the memory of his friend.

> "Dum memor ipse mei
> Dum
> Spiritus hos regit artus
> A————o————N
> 1772"

Bute was a man of scholarly tastes, and imbued with a love of science and literature and the fine arts. When Dutens visited him at Luton in 1773, he found that his library consisted of thirty thousand volumes. His cabinet of mathematical instruments and astronomical and philosophical apparatus was considered one of the most complete in Europe. He was deeply interested in floriculture and published a splendid work on botany in nine quarto volumes. Two of the groups classified by Linnaeus and Sir William Jones, *Stewartia* and *Butea*, were named after him. To him also Haller inscribed his celebrated *Bibliotheca Botanica*. The invaluable collection of about thirty thousand pamphlets, published at the time of the Commonwealth, which forms one of the most precious treasures of the British Museum, had been purchased by Bute for his own library, and it was bought from him by the King for presentation to the nation. Lady Louisa Stuart, Bute's daughter, speaking of her father's interest in chemistry and mineralogy, says that he would often have " Mr Wolf, an eminent chymist," in the house for weeks together.

Bute was not only interested in literature himself; he was also a conscientious patron of literary and scientific merit in others. Boswell says that the accession of George the Third opened a new and brighter prospect to men of literary merit, who had been honoured with no mark of royal favour in the preceding reign. To this result Bute's influence undoubtedly contributed. Dutens speaks of the secret assistance, which he rendered to poverty-stricken artists. Even Walpole admits that he extended his patronage to artists and men of letters, especially to those who hailed from his native land.

Mallet, Smollett, Macpherson and Home alike profited by the kindness of their powerful countryman.

> "The mighty Home, bemired in prose so long,
>   Again shall stalk upon the stilts of song;
> While bold MacOssian, wont in ghosts to deal,
>   Bids candid Smollett from his coffin steal."

Doctor Johnson owed his pension of three hundred pounds a year to the Prime Minister, who hailed from the country he abused so much. It is to Bute's credit that the pension was not given to Johnson as an inducement to write in support of the administration. The Minister expressly said to him, " It is not given you for anything you are to do, but for what you have done." Bute procured a pension for Thomas Sheridan, who had addressed to him the plan of a pronouncing dictionary, which he proposed to produce. It was this act on the part of the Minister which evoked Johnson's famous remark, "What! have they given him a pension? Then it is time for me to give up mine,"—a remark which, although subsequently modified, ended the friendship between Sheridan and Johnson. Jonas Hanway, the patriotic London merchant and philanthropist, who first carried an umbrella in the streets of London, was appointed by Bute one of the commissioners for victualling the Navy. Doctor Hill, who, after he received the Swedish Order of Vasa from Gustavus the Third, was commonly known as Sir John Hill, was one of the objects of Bute's bounty. Adam Ferguson, the historian of Rome and the friend of Sir Walter Scott's boyhood, who had been chaplain to the Forty-Second Regiment, was private tutor in the family of Bute from 1757 to 1759, when he became Professor of Natural Philosophy in Edinburgh University. It was Bute who introduced Fenning, the author of the Royal Dictionary to George III, and he is said to have written the introduction to the Dictionary, which was published in 1756. He is even found adding to the Collections of Dr William Hunter, the famous anatomist, by sending him "a singular fish from the Cape—he expects it to have some affinity to the frog fish."

John Home, the author, was one of the most intimate friends of Bute. Originally minister of the parish of Athelstaneford in the Church of Scotland, he amused his leisure by writing the tragedy of *Douglas*. The indignation evoked amongst his brother clerics by the appearance of his play, compelled him in 1757 to resign his charge. Soon after his resignation he became private secretary to Bute, who regarded him with a warm and fraternal affection. Home continued his dramatic authorship in his new sphere of duties, and, when his play of *Agis* was brought out by Garrick at Drury Lane in 1758, Bute took Prince George to see it more than once. Bute appointed the dramatist to the sinecure office of Conservator of Scots Privileges at Campvere, a post which, before it became a sinecure, was a sort of Scottish Consulate in Holland. With Bute's retirement, Home ceased to be his secretary, but he always remained his friend and correspondent.

Bute was willing to help even pronounced Jacobites. It was through his instrumentality that Sir James Stewart Denham, the Jacobite political economist, who had been obliged to fly from the country on account of his participation in the Rising of 1745, received a pardon in 1758. He invited Sir Robert Strange, who had been "out" in "the Forty-five," to engrave portraits of Prince George and himself. Strange, however, refused, probably as the result of political motives. Bute never forgave him for his action, and for years Strange was ignored by the Court, although he made every effort to recover the favour of his Sovereign. In 1775 he protested against his treatment in a book entitled *An Enquiry into the Rise and Establishment of the Royal Academy of Arts*, which is preceded by a dedicatory letter to the Earl of Bute, occupying nearly half the volume. He was ultimately forgiven, and in 1787 he was knighted. As far back as 1740 Bute appointed James Stewart of Kinwhinleck, a professed Jacobite, to the living of Kingarth in the Island of Bute. This cleric preferred to pray for the exiled Stuart family rather than for George II, but he was an eccentric man, and was compelled to resign his charge in 1754. It is perhaps not surprising that the charge of Jacobitism was one of those levelled at Bute.

In distributing his patronage, Bute professed to be guided by the maxim *detur digniori*—"let it be given to the more worthy." On 2nd July 1761, for example, he writes to his friend and henchman, Baron Mure :—

" Dear Mure, I have received your letter, with your double application. One of them seems made *par manière d'acquit*, because he was your relation. You might save yourself trouble in such cases, by assuring the person at once, that, though Lord Bute has the greatest friendship for you, he, in things of public concern, will neither regard your relation nor his own one minute, but turn his thought solely to a worthy subject....I repeat once more, and beseech you would attend to it ; merit and efficiency will ever weigh with me for publick office before private considerations. Adieu, dear Mure. Yours, Bute."

CHAPTER IX

IT has already been stated that Bute's enemies maintained that, though figuring as a patron of learning and a polite scholar, he possessed but a trifling stock of erudition. Lord Waldegrave said that he was anxious to be thought learned, but never succeeded, except with those who were exceedingly ignorant. Waldegrave added that his historical knowledge was chiefly taken from tragedies, wherein he was very deeply read, and that his classical learning extended no further than a French translation. Some of his enemies even sneered at his spelling. " The Earl," wrote Horace Walpole, " had so little knowledge and so little taste, that his own letters grew a proverb for want of orthography." One contemporary sums up the views of Bute's opponents as to his scholarship in a passage that is worth re-producing. " Bookish without learning," he says, " in his library of parade, as insensible and unconversable on the great objects of literature as one deaf and dumb questioned on a concert of music; as little of a judge as a blind man in a gallery of pictures. A dabbler in the fine arts, without grace, without taste. A traveller through countries without seeing them, and totally un-acquainted with his own. In a dull ungenial solitude, muddling away what leisure he may have from false politics, and ruinous counsels, in stuffing his portfolios with penny prints and pretty pictures of coloured simples, those gazing-traps of simpletons, and garnishing his knicknackatory with mechanical toys, baubles, and gimcracks, or varying his nonsense with little tricks of chemistry, while all these futile puerilities have been rendered still more futile by the gloom of a solemn visage, ridiculously exhibiting the preternatural character of a grave child."

Bute, not unnaturally, tried to interest the King in the artistic and scientific pursuits, to which he was himself devoted. This attempt on his part was laughed and sneered at. "The favourite," said Horace Walpole, " who had notions of honour, and was ostentatious, endeavoured to give a loftier cast to the disposition of his pupil, though not to the disparagement of the vassalage in which he was to be kept. Lord Bute had a little reading, and affected learning. Men of genius, the arts and artists, were to be countenanced. The arts might amuse the young King's solitary hours : authors might defend the measures of government, and were sure to pay for their pensions with incense, both to their passive and active protectors. The pedantry and artifice of these shallow views served but to produce ridicule. Augustus fell asleep over drawings and medals, which were pushed before him every evening : and Maecenas had so little knowledge and so little taste, that his own letters grew a proverb for want of orthography ; and the scribblers he countenanced, were too destitute of talents to raise his character or their own. The coins of the King were the worst that had appeared for above a century ; and the revenues of the Crown were so soon squandered in purchasing dependants, that architecture, the darling art of Lord Bute, was contracted from the erection of a new palace, to altering a single door-case in the drawing-room at St James's."

Conflicting testimony makes it difficult to get at the real truth as to Bute's accomplishments, but it is probable that he was a man of considerable information and scholarship. Lord Shelburne admits that he read a great deal, chiefly "out of the waybooks of science and pompous poetry." He states that Bute possessed "a great deal of superficial knowledge, such as is commonly to be met with in France and Scotland, chiefly upon matters of natural philosophy, mines, fossils, a smattering of mechanics, a little metaphysics, and a very false taste in everything." Shelburne gives us one piece of information that is interesting. He tells us that Lucan was his favourite poet among the ancients, and Queen Elizabeth's Earl of Essex his favourite author and object of imitation. He admired the letters of the Elizabethan noble and had them almost by heart. Bute's admiration of Lucan and Essex raises him in our estimation. The silent Scotsman did after all cherish ideals under his reserved exterior and retained in his soul some appreciation of romance. Dutens speaks in the highest terms of Bute's knowledge, and says that he never knew a man with whom one could be so long *tête-à-tête* without being tired. As for the reflections on his orthography, a glance at those of Bute's letters to Baron Mure in the *Caldwell Papers* which have been literally transcribed, show that the statement of Horace Walpole is a gross exaggeration. Bute wrote "oblidged," "benefet," "feell," "Christmass," but Walpole himself wrote "memoire" and "morow." Bute's spelling was no worse than that of other politicians of his age. Even the great Chatham wrote "adressed" and "doz" (for "does").

Bute's disposition was cold and severe. Horace Walpole states that he was too haughty to admit any to his familiarity but half a dozen authors and flatterers. "Sir Henry Erskine, a military poet; Home, a tragedy-writing parson; and Worseley, a rider of the great horse and architect, were his principal confidents." Bute was entirely devoid of the geniality and *savoir faire*, which are so valuable in the government of men, and especially in the management of popular assemblies. Who can estimate what Palmerston gained by his cheerful *cameraderie*, and freedom from stiffness? Who can say what Peel lost by his icy manner, and that smile, which Daniel O'Connell said was like the silver plate on a coffin? It is said that even in the interior of his family Bute was austere, harsh, difficult of access, and sometimes totally inaccessible even to his own children. He gave his full confidence to none, and consequently had few friends, for no man, as Lord Chesterfield says, thinks himself bound by a half confidence. In ordinary intercourse, he was proud, sullen, and unconciliatory. He never looked at those to whom he spoke, or who spoke to him—an ungracious habit, of which Lord Chesterfield said that if it hindered him from being penetrated, it equally hindered him from penetrating others.

He was a handsome man, and possessed a leg of unrivalled symmetry. Like Sir Willoughby Patterne in Meredith's romance, *The Egoist*, he found it a valuable weapon in the battle of life. "Our cavalier's is the poetic leg," says Meredith, "a portent, a valiance. He has it as Cicero had a tongue. It is a lute to scatter songs to his mistress; a rapier, is she obdurate." To Bute's leg his contemporaries ascribed much of his influence over the King's mother. Horace Walpole says he took every opportunity of displaying it, and more especially to the " poor captivated Princess."

Lord Waldegrave has left it on record that Bute affected a theatrical air of great importance. He was always upon stilts, says Lord Shelburne, never natural except now and then upon the subject of women. " There is an extraordinary appearance of wisdom," wrote Waldegrave, " both in his look and manner of speaking ; for whether the subject be serious or trifling, he is equally pompous, slow, and sententious." When he spoke on the Cider Tax, his delivery was so slow and solemn, that Charles Townshend, standing on the steps of the throne, said in an audible whisper, " Minute guns." The Reverend Alexander Carlyle, minister of Inveresk, gives an idea of the effect produced by Bute's manner, in his description of his first interview with him in 1758. He was accompanied by Robert Adam, the architect, and Bute received them booted and spurred and very coldly. When they left, Adam fell a cursing and swearing. What ! he exclaimed, had he been presented to all the princes in Italy and France, and most graciously received, to come and be treated with such pride and distance by the youngest Earl but one in all Scotland ! They were better friends afterwards, however, adds Carlyle, and Adam found Bute a kind patron, when his professional merit was made known to him. Carlyle himself subsequently met Bute riding in Hyde Park. They accompanied one another for half an hour, and had a very agreeable talk together. But he was, says Carlyle, a different man when he received audiences.

The strong bias displayed by Bute towards the

Scots has been already noticed. He did much to help
his countrymen in their struggles for place and fortune
in England. Alexander Wedderburn, to take a single
instance, largely owed it to the early assistance of Bute
that he became Lord Chancellor and Earl of Rosslyn.
It was through Bute's influence that he was returned as
Member of Parliament for the Ayr Burghs, and his
attachment to the Scottish minister brought down upon
him the lash of Churchill. In Dr Johnson's eyes, Bute's
partiality for the Scots was one of his chief faults.
Talking with Boswell one Good Friday at breakfast,
before going to church, the sage complained that Bute
turned out Dr Nichols, a very eminent man, from being
physician to the King, to make room for one of his
own countrymen, a man very low in his profession. He
said that Bute did wrong in employing Scotsmen to
go on errands for him, and in suffering them at his
levees to take priority of admittance over the first people
in England.

It is a curious fact that, in spite of his partiality for
Scotsmen, Bute never went to Scotland in later life.
There is a story that Bute accompanied George the
Third on a trip through part of Scotland in 1759. It
is stated by Mr Lewis Melville in his book, *Farmer
George*, that Bute and George paid visits to Edinburgh,
Glasgow, the Isle of Bute and a few other places,
accompanied only by two servants and preserving the
strictest incognito. This is at variance with a statement
made by Lord Rosebery, who says in his book on Pitt
that George the Third never travelled farther than
York. The present writer asked Lord Rosebery for
his opinion on the matter, and he replied, "There is not
the slightest proof of his ever having crossed the border

into Scotland, nor would it seem possible that he had ever done so, for every day in his life must have been chronicled." Mr Lewis Melville informed the present writer that his authority for his statement was a compilation entitled *George the Third, his Court and Family, a New Edition*, 1824, ascribed to John Galt. The authority does not appear a reliable one, and there can be little doubt that Lord Rosebery's view is correct.

Bute's relations to his native country during his tenure of power were interesting. In the eighteenth century it was the custom to hand the government of Scotland over to one particular minister, who was at once the representative of Scotland to the Administration and the representative of the Administration to Scotland. From 1725 to 1761, Scotland was administered by Archibald, third Duke of Argyll, who was nicknamed "King of Scotland." In April 1761, the Duke of Argyll died, and the government of Scotland passed to his nephew, Bute. "The crown of Scotland, too, has fallen on Bute's head," said Horace Walpole on Argyll's death. Bute committed the administration of Scotland to his brother, Stuart Mackenzie, who was appointed Lord Privy Seal of Scotland. Mackenzie had charge of it until 1765, when the enmity against his family drove him from office. On the retirement of Mackenzie, the government of Scotland was restored to the direct line of the Campbells, and passed into the hands of the Marquis of Lorne. Mackenzie, while in power, was assisted in exercising the duties and dispensing the patronage of *sous-ministre* by William Mure of Caldwell. Mure, who had originally commended himself to Bute by his able management of the Bute estates, became one of the Barons of the Scottish Court of Exchequer and Receiver-General of Jamaica. Mure, who during the Bute *régime* was naturally one of the most influential men in Scotland, lived in an old villa at Abbeyhill, Edinburgh, which had been occupied at different times by the Jacobite Duchesses of Gordon and Perth. "This," says Chambers, "was of course in its turn the *Court* of Scotland; and from the description of a gentleman old enough to remember attending the levees, I should suppose that it was as much haunted by suitors of all kinds as ever were the more elegant halls of Holyrood House."

The extent of Bute's political abilities is not easily ascertainable. Frederick, Prince of Wales, once observed that he was a fine showy man, and would make an excellent ambassador in a Court where there was no business. George the Third, on the other hand, said that Lord Mansfield had once assured him that he never knew any one who came so late into business, take to it, and do it so well. It is undoubtedly true that his first speech in the House of Lords greatly surprised the world, which had not been prepared for the high level of ability which Bute then showed. The probability is that Bute was a man of considerable capacity, who, if he had received a proper and gradual political training, would have made an able and competent public servant. There have undoubtedly been ministers who, without previous experience, have been placed in supreme power by the fiat of a monarch, and who, having only that monarch to please, have proved capable and successful rulers. But Bute had to control a complicated and elaborate system of government. He had to manage two Houses of Parliament, and he had to face a powerful phalanx of high-born opponents, who could only be overcome by constitutional methods. He had formed fine theories as to the duties of a minister, but contact with actual life showed him that theory and practice were two totally different things. Lord Shelburne in an interesting passage has dwelt upon this aspect of Bute's character. "He panted for the Treasury," says Shelburne, "having a notion that the King and he understood it from what they had read about revenue and funds, while they were at Kew. He had likewise an idea of great reformations, which all men who read the theory of things, and especially men who look up at being ministers, and want to remove and lower those that are, make a great part of their conversation. He had likewise a confused notion of rivalling the Duc de Sully, all which notions presently vanished when he came to experience the difficulties of it, and to find that dealing with mankind was the first thing necessary, of which he began to find himself entirely incapable." Doctor Johnson dwelt upon the same defect in Bute's character in a conversation with Boswell. "Lord Bute," he said, "though a very honourable man—a man who meant well—a man who had his blood full of prerogative—was a theoretical statesman—a book minister —and thought this country could be governed by the influence of the crown alone....Lord Bute took down too fast, without building up something new." "Because, Sir," said Boswell, "he found a rotten building. The political coach was drawn by a set of bad horses; it was necessary to change them." "But," replied Johnson, "he should have changed them one by one." And on another occasion he observed of Lord Bute, "It was said of Augustus, that it would have been better for Rome

that he had never been born, or had never died. So
it would have been better for this nation, if Lord Bute
had never been minister, or had never resigned." Bute
was not supported by men of character and ability such
as were to be found among the Whigs. The long
exclusion of the Tories from office had prevented the
development of official experience and capacity on the
Tory side. Bute had to rely on incompetent men like
Dashwood and unscrupulous men like Fox. The
conditions amidst which he found himself united to
make the work of government difficult and hazardous.
Above all, it must be remembered that, in all the
accusations of incompetence which were made against
him, ample allowance must be made for party bitterness.
Lady Louisa Stuart, Bute's daughter, relates that Wilkes
was once asked by Lord Sheffield why he so hated
Bute. "Hate him?" said the demagogue, "no such
thing. I had no dislike to him as a man, and I thought
him a good minister, but it was my game to attack and
abuse him."

George the Third complained to George Rose that
Bute was lacking in political firmness, but, when the
circumstances are considered, the enormous difficulty
of his position may excuse his not persisting in his
thankless task. The lack of support from his followers,
the intense hostility of the people, the opposition of Pitt
and the Whigs, and possibly the waning confidence of
his master, might well have unnerved a much abler and
more experienced minister. Bute made an honest
attempt to govern the country on Tory principles, and
he failed because the Whigs were too strong. If it was
a crime to be a Tory when Whiggism was dominant,
then Bute was a criminal. But apart from his political

views, if the prejudices against him as a Scot and an alleged intimate of the Princess Augusta, are put aside, there is nothing in Bute's character that entitles either the historian or the politician to make him the object of his contempt or scorn.   Amidst the Newcastles and the Rockinghams, and the Whig figureheads who so long governed England, Bute stands out as an interesting and almost pathetic figure.   He certainly does not merit the scornful language in which so many writers have spoken of his character and career.

LIST OF THE PRINCIPAL AUTHORITIES
USED BY THE AUTHOR

Memoirs of the Life and Reign of George III, by J. H. Jesse, 1867.

Memoirs of the Reign of George III, by Horace Walpole, 1894.

William Pitt, Earl of Chatham, by Albert von Ruville, translated by Chaytor, 1907.

History of England, by Lord Mahon, vols. IV, V, and VI, 1858.

The Grenville Papers, 1853.

Anecdotes of the Earl of Chatham, 1794.

Lives of the Lord Chancellors, by Lord Campbell, 4th. ed., 1856-7.

Lady Mary Wortley Montagu and Her Times, by George Paston, 1907.

Memoirs of the Reign of George II, by Horace Walpole, 1846.

Historical Memoirs, by Wraxall, 1836.

Lady Louisa Stuart, Selections from Her Manuscripts, edited by Home, 1899.

Life of the Earl of Shelburne, by Fitzmaurice, 1875.

Memoirs of Lord Waldegrave, 1821.

Memoirs of the Administration of Pelham, by Coxe, 1829.

Sybil, by Disraeli.

Diaries and Correspondence of George Rose, 1860.

Life of Lord Chancellor Hardwicke, by Harris, 1847.

Farmer George, by Lewis Melville, 1907.

Memoirs of Lord Rockingham, by Lord Albemarle, 1852.

The North Briton.

The Letters of Horace Walpole.

Chatham's Correspondence, 1838-40.

History of England, by Adolphus, 1802.

Caricature History of the Georges, by Wright, 1867.

Anecdotes of Himself, by Hogarth, 1833.
History of England in the Eighteenth Century, by Lecky, 1878.
Early History of C. J. Fox, by Trevelyan, 1880.
Life of Johnson by Boswell.
The Bedford Correspondence, 1842–6.
The Caldwell Papers (Maitland Club), 1854.
Charles Macklin, by Parry, 1891.
Poetical Works of Charles Churchill, 1892.
Records of My Life, by John Taylor, 1832.
Life and Times of Lord Brougham, by Himself, 1871.
Memoirs of Moore, by Earl Russell, 1853–6.
Bishop Newton's Autobiography, 1782.
The Letters of Lord Chesterfield.
Memorials of C. J. Fox, by Earl Russell, 1853–7.
Memoirs of Thomas Hollis, by Blackburne, 1780.
Life of Home, by Henry Mackenzie, in Home's Works, 1822.
Gleanings from an Old Portfolio, edited by Mrs Clark, 1895–8.
Burke, by Morley, 1906.
Pitt, by Rosebery, 1898
Anecdotes of Some Distinguished Persons, by Seward, 1795–7.
Thoughts on the Present Discontents, by Burke, 1770.
Walpoliana, Anecdotes collected by Horace Walpole, 1799.
George the Third as Man, Monarch, and Statesman, by Beckles
      Willson, 1907.
Personal and Party Government, by D. A. Winstanley, 1910.
Sheridan, by Fraser Rae, 1896.
Memoirs of Robert Strange, by Dennistoun, 1855.
Letters of Lady Louisa Stuart to Miss Clinton, edited by Home,
      1901–3.
Autobiography of Alexander Carlyle, 1860.
Traditions of Edinburgh, by Chambers, 1868.
A Century of Scottish History, by Craik, 1901.
Scottish Men of Letters in the Eighteenth Century, by Graham,
      1901.
Political History of England, vol. x (1760–1801), by Hunt, 1905.
Bute in the Olden Time, by Hewison, 1894–5.
Dictionary of National Biography.

INDEX

Printed in the United States
By Bookmasters